Secrets of a
Phone Sex Operator

Secrets of a Phone Sex Operator

The Bizarre—and
Often Hilarious—Reality at the
Other End of the Line

Stacey Weiss

Illustrated by: Dennis Phelps

Library of Congress Control Number:		2010918567
ISBN:	Hardcover	978-1-4568-3303-9
	Softcover	978-1-4568-3302-2
	Ebook	978-1-4568-3304-6

This book was printed in the United States of America.

To order additional copies of this book, contact:
Xlibris Corporation
1-888-795-4274
www.Xlibris.com
Orders@Xlibris.com
91545

Contents

DEDICATION:

I have to dedicate this book to all the clients I have ever had. Without them, I would never have been able to write this book.

"Abandon the Search for Truth, Settle for a Good Fantasy"
—Author Unknown

CHAPTER ONE:
How I Got Started

> **PHONE ACTRESS**
> Seeking women with sexy
> voices, must be 18 years
> or older. If you think you
> have what it takes, leave a
> message and if we like
> your voice, we'll call you
> back.
> 7 02-XXX-XXXX

I've always been a sexually charged woman. That may seem like an obvious thing to say; after all, human beings are hard wired to have sex, to procreate. But some people aren't all that sexually driven. In fact, some people could care less how much sex they've had in the past week, month, or even year. So when I say "charged," I mean it. Sex drives me. I like sex. I like sex for myself, but I also like it for others. I like it when someone gets off because of me and I like getting off because of someone else. It's a give-and-take situation, and it works well. Some people would frown on this. Some would call it a sexual addiction or call me a nympho, but for me, it simply is what it is.

Unfortunately, in this day and age, there are very, very unsafe ways of being overly sexually active. This is why I'm thankful I fell into the career that I did, rather than being driven somewhere completely out in left field by my overactive hormones.

Nearly everyone has had some form of phone sex in their lives, whether as teenagers just learning how things go, as young adults, or even middle aged. We've all done it to some extent, even if it's jokingly, a little light teasing, or deeper, more developed and intricate descriptions that go way beyond what we'd normally do in "real life." Why we do it is another question. It's safe, and/or it's fun, we're bored, lonely or just plain frustrated, or we just want a little fun that's totally free of ties—free of the normal societal constraints. After all, a phone sex operator knows what the guy is calling for and she doesn't expect him to be there in morning.

I started having phone sex about the same time in my life as most everyone else and with the person most everyone else has it with: in my teens, with my boyfriend. Then of course, I had phone sex with several boyfriends after that. One of them even said to me: "You could get paid for this, you're so good," all I thought was, "who in hell would pay for something like that." And the thought was just pushed aside or shelved in the deeper recesses of my brain.

I moved to Las Vegas when I was 21 years old and like most people who move on a whim and find themselves broke, I was in search for a second job to pay the bills. Shortly into my first year in Vegas, I decided to answer an ad for a "Phone Actress" position. As naive as I was at the time, I had absolutely no inkling as to what it meant.

It was a small ad in a free paper that read "Call and leave a message. If we like your voice, we will call you back." I picked up the phone and dialed, and while my normal voice is not all that sexy, this mysterious other voice came out as I left my message, one much more soothing and sexier. The next day, to my amazement, I received a call back.

"Hello, is this Stacey?", asked the voice of a young sounding woman on the other line. I answered yes, as calmly as I could, fearful my voice would crack, because I had absolutely no idea what this job was about.

"This is Veronica. I'm calling on behalf of XXX Company, to let you know we received your voicemail yesterday and would like to discuss the details of the position."

I believe I squeaked out something like, "Oh, good!"

"We are a phone sex company, and the ad you answered was for a phone sex operator. Do you have any experience in phone sex?", she asked me.

I was floored. I told her that I had only personal experience with boyfriends, trying to retain that new, smooth voice I'd discovered the day before. "Not a problem. Would you like me to explain the details of the position?", she said, so calm and collected, like she had asked that question a million times before.

I stammered something else and she continued. The job was fairly simple: phone calls from guys who called the company would be sent directly to my phone at the times I was signed on to take them. All I had to do was pick up the phone and do whatever it took to please them.

She went on to tell me the types calls I could expect to be getting, what type of hours I needed to work and how much I would get paid. She then told me that I would be receiving a packet via e-mail that had all the information I needed to start working right away.

I waited, excited and apprehensive, for the packet to arrive. I had paid to get packets before for "work at home" businesses, but this one was free and seemed totally legit. It came within minutes and I filled it out and headed to Kinko's to fax it back.

The next day, Veronica called me again, in her sweet and young voice, and said that all I had to do was call in to the company and ask to be signed on. At the time, I decided to go by the name Faith for my fantasy girl. Faith was the person I really wanted to look like: 5-foot-3-inches tall, 120 pounds, curly brown hair with blond highlights, brown eyes, and 32B breasts. In that manner, phone sex can be just as much a fantasy for the operator as for the caller. I was able to completely reinvent myself, someone who would take on a life of her own, with a different yet similar past, her own sexual history and a plethora of kinky stories.

I called later that night to sign on for my first shift, and thus, so swiftly, began my career in the phone sex industry.

CHAPTER TWO:
And So It Began

My First Few Calls

So there I was, lying in bed watching TV, my phone next to me, waiting, actually quite impatiently, for my first phone call to come in. When the phone finally did ring, I perked up in bed and grabbed it, my heart thumping. Veronica was on the other end. "I've got a caller for you. His name is Bob K. He chose you based on your description from the website." Mentally calming myself, I told her OK, and she hung up, instantly connecting me to Bob.

Of course, I had been rehearsing all day, hat I was going to say, how I was going to introduce myself, how I was going to handle a variety of desires. I thought I could easily imagine most of the things guys would ask for. How wrong I was! How naive! I couldn't possibly imagine the depths of human fantasy.

A deep voice said "Hello?" I immediately answered, "Hi there Bob. How are you doing today?" The conversation went just the way I expected it to: nearly the same as I had talked to most of my boyfriends in the past. It was simple and made me feel very confident. And to be honest, the call was pretty hot. It made me wet to go over all the details of how I would please him. I laid back in my bed, closed my eyes and imagined myself actually doing what I was telling him, just instead of him, I imagined one of my ex-boyfriends. That made it very easy and probably why it made me so wet. I didn't cum talking to him, mostly because it was only 10 minutes, but I did enjoy myself. At the end of the call, he told me it was great and he would be calling back.

In hindsight, I knew he would call back, of course, because I was so into it. The operator must, at the very least, appear to be into the call and not simply making noises. Even the most unresponsive and quiet guys can tell when the chick on the other end isn't really paying attention. It isn't that the operator necessarily needs to be getting wet every time, but she must be engaged and be a good actress. Who knows what kinds of girls this guy had talked to before, but in my newness and eagerness, I must have been a breath of fresh air.

A few more calls came in that night that were pretty straight forward and what I would call vanilla sex. Then, as the night wore on, I had a couple that were more kinky than what I was used to. One guy wanted me to role-play that I was the babysitter of his kids and he wanted to drive me home and have me come on to him.

I surprised myself with role-playing. It was easy—surprisingly easy. Maybe that was due, in part, to me being Faith and not myself. I was already acting, so what was acting a little more in comparison to that? I had honestly always wanted to be an actress, but knew I wasn't good looking enough to be in the movies, so maybe this form of acting was perfect for me. I found myself anxious to see what other scenarios the guys would come up with.

That night I made $50. I was signed on for just a few hours. I had the next day free from my day job and I was ready and anxious and excited for more.

Hard Lessons Learned

The next day, I got cocky. This scary thing of phone sex with complete strangers was coming (forgive the pun) so easily to me and making me money so quickly, I think I got over-confident.

That day, I spoke with a guy named Nick, a sweet, lonely guy who just wanted to imagine being with a woman who cared for him. We had about an hour-long conversation and talked for more than half of it about random things that were going on in both our lives. An hour-long conversation in the phone sex business that doesn't involve sex is actually not that unusual by the way. On the other hand, most guys know they're being charged by the minute, so they tend to delve straight into the nitty-gritty or only chit chat for a few minutes in the beginning of the conversation. They go for what they want, figuring the bigger bang for their buck, the better.

In hindsight, I can see what Nick wanted was a girlfriend or what we refer to as "the girlfriend experience," not blatant phone sex. He should have been on a dating site, not on the phone, spending money every minute. But, I let it continue because it was easy money and honestly, was doing something for me, too. I had gone through some rough breakups and boyfriends who didn't treat me well, so it was nice to hear a guy tell me how much he enjoyed our conversation and spending time with me, even if it was only on the phone.

Nick ended up calling me back a few times that day, and a few more times the next couple of days, totaling probably about six hours of talk time, the majority of it rarely about sex. When we did talk about sex, I did masturbate with him, and we would cum together. I got wrapped up in the whole thing, the romanticism of it all. To make things worse, I was in Las Vegas, and he was in Ely, which was only four hours away.

I have been doing phone sex for seven years at the writing of this book, and I preach to everyone NOT to meet their clients because I know what can happen. Simply put, I know from firsthand experience.

Nick told me he wasn't gorgeous, but that he was a good looking guy, at about 5'5" and 170 pounds. I felt so comfortable with him that I told him my real name and even what I really looked like. We were getting along so well that, when he repeatedly insisted that I take his phone number and e-mail address, I caved and took them, a huge no-no in the phone sex industry. You never give personal information, nor do you accept it. And if you do accept it, you're just pretending to take it to make them happy. It's not only unsafe to do so, but it's also considered undercutting the business you're working for, something that can certainly get you fired if they monitor calls. It's essentially stealing a client, something that is written into every contract. I had signed a similar contract with XXX Company.

I called Nick a couple of times over the next few nights, outside my normal working hours. We got along so well; he was romantic and sweet and very nice to me. Over the course of a week, I was so drawn into what he was saying that I agreed to drive all the way out to Ely and stay with him for the weekend.

As I drove the long four hours, the emotional turmoil was excruciating. I was excited about meeting this incredible man, but also nervous; after all, I was on my way to meet a complete stranger whom I'd only talked to over a phone sex hotline. He could be a total nutcase. To make matters worse, I had agreed to meet him at his apartment and not a public place and none of my friends knew where I was going because I knew they would kill me if I told them the truth. So if something happened, it meant they would have no idea where I was.

What if he was a serial killer? What if he raped me? What if he was a convicted felon? Even with all of those thoughts running through my head, I was determined to keep a positive attitude. We'd spoken for a long amount of time, so I figured we knew each other well enough. If we had met in a bar, and I went home with him, I could have known even less of him. It wasn't going to turn into some sort of horrible news story the next day. He would be just as awesome as he was on the phone. I told myself these things, over and over.

I got lost on the drive there. Ely was far, it was late, and I was tired emotionally, mentally, and physically. I called him to stay awake, to bolster my confidence that this would work out OK, and to get directions. So I was on the phone with him when I pulled up to his apartment.

He should have heard the stutter in my words the moment I saw him, the way my sentence trailed off to a dead stop, but he didn't pay any attention. He was waiting outside his apartment, and I was floored. My headlights flashed over a man on his cell phone, except the man couldn't possibly be Nick. Then the man waved, and I nearly dropped the phone. He said hello into my ear. I was grateful for the darkness, as I'm sure my face was telling everything: the cold sensation running from my temples and down my spine, the shock, betrayal, fear, and bladder-crushing panic.

The man who I thought was 5'5", 170 pounds, and "relatively fit," per his words, was actually closer to 270 pounds and very unfit. While I'm not a small girl and have nothing against larger men, I was very upset by the fact that he had lied to me, had lied to the point of getting me to drive four hours to see him. What did he expect would happen when I found out the truth? Did he think that I would gloss over the obvious lie and dive into his arms anyway?

Granted, as a phone sex operator, I had lied at first, but I had also come clean in the ensuing conversations with Nick. I hadn't stayed behind my facade in order to get him to like me more. The rage subsided quickly, though, as I turned off my car and sat for a moment in the darkness. Mostly what was replacing the anger was shame. I was ashamed that I had given in to what every instinct in my body had told me not to do.

I hung up the phone, collecting myself as he drew nearer in the dark. Taking a gulp of air to steady myself, I got out of the car.

"Nick?" He lurched into a lumbering run and enveloped me in a crushing hug followed by an awkward and slightly wet kiss that I just barely managed to get on my cheek instead of on the lips. "What do I do!?" ran through my head like a mantra as I forced a smile on my face. I had promised to come over and spend the weekend with him, and I just wanted to get back in the car and drive right back to Vegas.

His enthusiasm was overwhelming, like a large dog who's left outside every day and just finally got to come in. He literally bubbled with excitement, pulling on my hand, leading us toward his apartment, and I hesitantly followed, looking forlornly back at my car.

As we reached the steps up to his place, I couldn't imagine the situation getting much worse, but it soon would. He had told me he was 32 years old and "occasionally cared for" his mother. This, of course, meant he lived with her. It also apparently meant he didn't care for much else, as the apartment was a mess, and Mom was hollering something unintelligible from a back bedroom while the TV loudly blared commercials at us when we walked in. Nick, looking at me abashedly, yelled back at her, something like, "Ma, shut up! I've got company!" I cringed, expecting her to come barreling out of there, a larger, older, female version of him, but she stayed put and, surprisingly, shut up. Perhaps she was as surprised as I was that Nick had company.

He, of course, walked me straight back to his bedroom, still babbling and bubbling. I wouldn't have minded sitting for a moment in their gritty kitchen, having a glass of water, and getting to know this person I thought I'd known so well until now, but I wasn't given a chance at collecting myself. From the living room to the bed room, it went from bad to worse. Simply, there were porn videos everywhere and I'm talking boxes. Now, I don't mind a little porn, and have thoroughly enjoyed myself with it in the past, but the blatancy of it all blew me away: He was sad, just pathetic, and clearly all he wanted was sex in the flesh.

As though it hadn't been apparent enough, I realized why he was so lonely and calling a phone sex line for company. He'd driven off anyone else who would talk to him anymore. In a flash, I imagined this man's history: Kids making fun of him growing up. He was probably awkward in high school, but friendly enough. His attempts at fitting in probably involved going to school dances by himself, getting turned down for dances, dates, and even general overtures at friendship; being taunted and teased for his weight, his funny facial features, his manners and ways of talking; the boys looking at him like they didn't know what to do with him; the girls refusing to even do that. Briefly, very briefly, I felt bad for him. But then the rational part of my brain screamed, "He lied to you! He manipulated you!" I felt my features shut down, the false smile I'd glued in place falling away, my face turning to stone. I sat on the bed, cell phone in hand, my jacket still on. Nervous and appalled, I jerked to my feet as he made a move to sit next to me.

"I think this was a mistake. I should get going," was all I could blurt out, the words running together, feeling my face flush red with embarrassment and anger—anger about the lies, the manipulation, anger at him for putting me in this situation, for forcing me to take a stand. He stood there a moment, his gangly arms hanging loose by his sides, and I wondered at my options if he turned violent. There wasn't much I could do—he was between me and the door, his mother probably wouldn't help if I yelled, and the footing wasn't even very stable due to the clothes and porn and who knew what else on the floor. My brain decided to be helpful and run in circles, panicky. A sneaky sweat broke out on my forehead and I resisted the urge to wipe it away, resisted the urge to move at all, like a mouse pinned by a cat's stare. We stood that way for a good minute or two, as my anger deserted me and gave way to useless, mind-numbing fear. His silence began to scare me even more, and I convinced myself if I spoke—did anything at all, he would snap, his tenuous hold on his temper was that fragile, that barely in check. I couldn't look at him. All I could see was his body posture, upset, the shoulders rounded, the hands slightly curled next to his thighs, the awkwardly large feet turned slightly toward each other.

"I understand if you want to leave," he said, blurting just as much as I had. He looked so sad, not angry at all. It seemed my fear about him snapping was a result of my overactive imagination. I nodded, feeling bad again, so I reached out and gave him a big hug. I walked past him, I kept my head down, feeling so fucking bad, but at the same time, desperate to get out—get out and away as quickly as possible so I could pretend none of this ever happened, pretend I hadn't been so stupid. I hoped he would walk me to the door and leave me alone from there, but he accompanied me all the way to the car. We walked in complete silence, he really was a very nice person; just sad and a liar. He tried to hug me, but I pulled away, quickly swinging open the car door and ducking inside. As I backed out, I half-heartedly went to wave, but he was already walking away, like a dog that had been beaten and dumped on a deserted road. The guilt crashed into me, and then the anger came back, wave upon wave.

Needless to say, I went back to Las Vegas, a mess of emotions, but eventually relief won out. It could have been so much worse. I arrived at around 4 a.m. and went right to bed, vowing never to tell anyone about it. But the shame cut deepest the next day. What was I thinking? Meeting a complete stranger? At his house, no less? What would my friends say? What would my employer say? I remember pacing the house—it was a Saturday, only a week since I'd started the job—pacing and tearing myself up over the stupidity of it all.

In hindsight, of course, I recognize this experience for what it was: a very good lesson in what not to do as a phone sex operator. Never get personal. Never let it get that far, always play it off. But there's a balance to it: You can't be such a cold shoulder that the caller is hurt. You have to play it just right so they feel you still like them, still enjoy talking to them, but they never receive any true information, anything at all that could give them a hint as to who you really are. In short, you can tell them anything you like to keep them hooked, but, in reality, none of it is traceable back to you. You must always be Faith, never your true self.

The next day, after avoid taking any calls Saturday night, I gave myself a mental shake to get out of the funk. I couldn't keep shying away from this just because I'd been dumb about it the first week. I wondered how many other women had made the same mistake I did—and if the consequences were much more dire for them. I wasn't a singularity, I told myself; I needed to get back on the horse. Nick didn't attempt to contact me again, thankfully, or I would have had to change my number and e-mail. Instead, I assume he moved on just as I did. I shook it off and gave it another try, this time approaching my new job as it really was: just another job.

I had to maintain the maturity, the upper hand in essence, and stay above it all. My approach before was total immersion, and while it was effective with the callers, it was obviously a tad bit too effective, too convincing for the both of us. Thus, I learned in a quick crash-course of a week how a good phone sex operator, well, operates: She is an actor, through and through. Good actors can often make their viewers really believe who they are trying to portray. But good actors also never forget who they really are. I was not Faith, but Faith could and would give her all to every caller without really giving them anything but their own desires. Never hers.

The Reality of The Situation

After the Nick escapade, I stuck to a schedule with the job to help enhance the view that it was just a job, not something I needed to get worked up over every day. I continued taking calls after work on the week days and every weekend. Ultimately, after I got over berating myself, I found I was really enjoying the freedom the gig gave me, and the extra money, of course, didn't hurt. After a while—I think after Veronica started feeling more secure about me, trusting me more, relying on me more—I started receiving more and more of the "risque" callers; the guys who like things a little bit differently than most people. Some of them are very straight forward fantasies, the kinds we've all heard about one time or another but have never been interested in ourselves. Others, well, they're a little more out there. And some of them are WAY out there, beyond most of our imaginations.

The company called itself a "no restriction" company, allowing callers to talk about anything they wanted to—and I mean anything. Of course, I was told all of this up front, vocally and in writing, so I was warned. But some of the things still came as a shock—things like incest, bestiality, and even underage fantasies. Those are all heard of, at the least, but still a little shocking to my then-unprepared mind. Later on, of course, I was exposed to more.

There are many companies that deal with "no restrictions" and of course their comment to us PSOs is "we don't want to hear about it, it's up to you whether you talk about those fantasies or not." It's frowned upon by the general public to discuss such fantasies, but in the phone sex realm, sometimes, if you don't talk about them, you won't get calls. As far as whether I discuss these calls or not, well, no comment.

The key to dealing with this type of thing is accepting that, yes, these guys are "messed up"—yes, they have very taboo fantasies. But at the very least, they're calling a phone sex line and most likely aren't acting on these strange fantasies in reality. The hot line gave them an outlet and, once I realized that, the easier it became to shut down the part of my brain screaming, "What the fuck!?" and just go with the flow. As I say all the time: "I throw my morals out the window when I do phone sex."

That is, until I had my first extremely taboo call that ultimately made me question my decision to become a phone sex operator at all.

Larry had become a very regular caller by the first month or so of my entering the biz. He'd call me at least every other day. His fantasies started out relatively vanilla. As each call came in, they became progressively weirder until it all just came to a head.

We'd talk for about thirty minutes to an hour, discussing a role-play where I was a single mother who applied to work at his private business—a secretary position at his home office. As the single mother, I was desperately in need of a place to stay with my nine year-old daughter, and according to his fantasy, I was willing to do anything to stay at his home. This was all well and good, and I had no problem with his fantasy.

I see how he took pleasure from being the one in control, able to hold a place to live over my head to get what he wanted. But then the fantasy strayed into deeper waters, territory that made me start to feel really uncomfortable.

It started out with light abuse and torture to "me," the secretary living in his home. He would force me to be naked at all times, answering calls for his business, sitting at the desk he'd set up for me, etc. Then he began smacking my ass, and telling me I couldn't object or it would get worse. Of course, it got worse—the smacking progressed to hitting my tits, and then it began to get really weird, with burning my breasts on the stove. Of course I went along with his fantasy and would pretend to moan and groan in pain. After a few minutes of each progression of his roleplay (toward the end of the 30 minutes) he'd say, "We're done for the day. I'll call again soon."

To top all this off, he told me if I didn't let him do these increasingly bizarre things to me then he would rape my daughter. Then it progressed to him forcing me to do things to my daughter on the promise that he wouldn't do them if I did. In his fantasy, I had to scream and cry and pretend to really be in pain. Because I didn't want my neighbors to get concerned, I would sometimes have to sit in a closet of my apartment, so that I could muffle my sounds. And sitting in the closet wasn't much fun. I had nothing to keep my mind occupied and distracted from his twisted fantasy. Nowadays, I don't have that problem, I play video games, chat online, do a puzzle, anything to keep me occupied while I talk to these guys. (It helps me to not fall asleep too!)

Needless to say, I was horribly disturbed with Larry's increasingly strange requests. But somehow, I kept myself calm—for the most part; outwardly, at any rate—and followed along with the roleplay. After each session, I signed off work for about an hour to collect myself—and then I'd start all over again, hoping not to get someone so perverted.

Of course, Larry would, more often than not, call the next day I signed on. I began to feel very hesitant about work—very sick to my stomach, sometimes even panicky, worse than I'd ever felt that night with Nick. The phone would ring and my heart would skip a beat, afraid the dispatcher would tell me that Larry was on the line. I could have called up the dispatcher and asked to not talk to Larry again, but since it was only my first month, I didn't want to make them think that I was being picky, and therefore had the luxury to block a caller. In fact, in all my years of phone sex, I have only blocked maybe a handful of callers.

Larry's fantasy progressed further to harsher torture, which I will not go into. Then it took one more step: He wanted me to seduce a man he despised, tie the man up in his office, tease him, get him hard by sucking his cock, bit his cock off then kill him by hitting him over the head with a paperweight. That did it. I don't know why nothing else did it until that point, but murder was definitely not anything near sexual in my mind—this was getting into psychotic territory. I almost hung up right there, but tried so desperately to keep my composure, knowing he was a regular client of the company, and I certainly didn't want to piss them off. I probably did shut down a little there, and from my standpoint now, I look down on that as a professional in this line of work. But, thankfully, Larry's fantasy was over for the day (he liked to drag things out), and he hung up a few minutes later. The second he was gone, I called out of work and drove to my then boyfriend's house, crying hysterically the whole way.

My boyfriend told me to quit. He was okay with the job, but he didn't like seeing what it did to me that day. I was a mess. While it was only a month or so in, it really was a turning point. It made me question whether I could really handle it, whether I had as strong a mind as I thought I did. I had read books about serial killers since high school and was at the time a criminal justice major at the University of Nevada: Las Vegas (UNLV), so I had heard and read some pretty messed up things that killers did to their victims. But it was totally different to actually hear it coming out of someone's mouth, especially in a sexual context. I kept thinking, "this sicko gets *turned on* by this stuff?" Is this something he's done to someone or really wants to do to someone? What if I make it sound so appealing, he decides to go out and actually do this to a woman?

I had no one to talk to about any of this, because at the time, no one knew what I did for a living aside from my close friends and my boyfriend. It was all on me; I had to decide if I could handle it. I sat back and thought to myself, "if I can read about these things serial killers have done to their victims and have even seen pictures, why can't I talk to this guy?" The goal with going into criminal justice was to become a criminal profiler and do studies on killers to learn why they did what they did. Maybe I could use this to my advantage. I could actually study my callers and ask them certain questions in order to get a better understanding of why they had the fantasies they had and where they came from. In this context, I was able to pull myself further from the personal aspect of the call and pick it apart instead. Like Nick, Larry was just another learning curve, another lesson learned on the way as I perfected Faith, my act, my cover, my protection, and above all, my self.

So I moved on, determined not only to be a phone sex operator but a psychologist of sorts with my callers. I listened and observed and analyzed the things they told me. At the same time, I was pushing the horrible stuff into the back of my head so that I wouldn't dwell on it. Hoping they kept it all to this phone call and never let it spill into reality. It's like watching a movie about someone dying and afterward thinking, "Wow, if I had to go through losing someone like that . . ." and then dwelling on it for days. Sometimes you have to stop yourself and say, "It's just a movie!" That's what I did: "It's just a fantasy! Now let it go!"

And while this next part took a few years to perfect, I have turned my mine into a virtual file cabinet of sorts. I imagine my mind just like that, that each caller has his folder, when he calls, I label it, and put his name, sound of his voice and his fantasy inside. When I hang up the call, I take the folder in my mind and put it back into the filing cabinet. When he calls back, for some reason, my mind is able to find that folder (I must file really well in there!), pull it out, and let me recall the information. I have actually been known to pull out information on clients I haven't talked to in a year, just by hearing their voice, and a snippet of their fantasy. With that, I can recall exactly what we talked about the last time. I just wish it would work in the rest of my life!

Moving On

I've always associated the word fantasy with good stuff, fun stuff. To me, fantasies are fun things you want to try; exciting, sexy things that benefit you or you and someone else, in new ways. Not scary, fucked up, shitty things you want to do to other people because it makes you feel better about yourself. The experiences with Nick and especially with Larry were both certainly eye openers. I felt so foolish looking at myself from just a few months prior, how I had perceived the world. In essence, the job made me grow up reall quick, practically over night. This isn't to say that fantasies are anything different to me now, but I realized that not everyone views the definition of the word itself the same. For a scary amount of people, the word fantasy is a selfishly driven experiment on others, either on how much you can get away with doing to them, or how far you can push them.

Since that call, I have taken tens of thousands of calls and dealt with fantasies that are even worse than Larry's, if you can imagine that. Some of these fantasies that make me question my morals, question humanity, question my sanity; but as I've had to say to myself over and over again, "if I wasn't there for them to talk to, what would they be doing? Where would they vent?" The other side of the coin is that these callers are sometimes the most lucrative ones I've got because of their reliability in calling back and willingness to spend as much as it takes to complete their fantasies.

Over the years, aside from the freaky stuff, I've also had some pretty interesting and honestly quite amusing calls. Some are so hilarious that I've just had to relate the non-specifics to others, or I'd burst. In fact, some of those calls are detailed later on. So it's not all terrible—don't get me wrong: There are some perks to being a phone sex operator.

CHAPTER THREE:
Ins and Outs

Stereotyping

The reason I mentioned Veronica's sweet and young voice earlier was to make somewhat of a point. A few months after I started working for XXX Company, they contacted me and asked if I would like to become a dispatcher because, like me, they were located in Las Vegas. Intrigued, I made an appointment with Veronica and drove about 20 minutes for my interview.

XXX Company's office complex was this tiny one-story building with only four other offices in a not-so-nice part of Las Vegas, and I was thankful it was daytime. The outside of the building was old and crumbling and hadn't been very well maintained. Their suite's front windows were blocked out by a poor tinting job. I tried the door, but it was locked. Within a minute, a larger woman, around 30, answered the door. She was very pretty, but probably over 200 pounds. When she opened the door, she said, "You must be Stacey," in that sweet and young voice I remembered from the phone interview. I was honestly shocked. Veronica sounded like she was only 18 years old, or possibly younger. It just goes to show how deceiving voices can be.

To make a long story short, I ended up getting the dispatching job. It meant, unfortunately, that I had to come back there every day and work from 8 a.m. to 4 p.m. That aside, it turned out to be a great opportunity for me because it taught me more about the inside workings of a phone sex company. It taught me a lot of things that I use today in my own business. I worked as a dispatcher and a PSO for a few months, but got a better paying day job, but kept up with the phone sex at night.

Again, Veronica wasn't as young and skinny as I had expected. Roughly 90 percent of the female phone sex operators I've met in person or via the internet, including the ones I've hired, have been larger, older women, with beautiful voices. In fact, most of the girls who play 18 and 19 year olds for me are in their 40s.

Unfortunately, the stereotype of phone sex operators is true—that we are larger women; that the girl you're talking to who sounds so young and thin and has a beautiful model's picture on her website, is probably a much larger woman who doesn't look anything like the model. It's sobering that most of us live up to the stereotype. I have seen some phone sex operators' websites with pictures that look as though they could be themselves, but who really knows? In fact, the picture I use as my model is an old friend of mine who is much more attractive. I do not use my actual picture—of course, this is also for safety reasons.

Who Am I? What Am I?

I've wondered sometimes how I should classify myself when describing what I do. Yes, I'm a phone sex operator, but I am not like a regular operator at a switchboard. I am not a slut because I charge, and sluts don't charge. Technically, I'm a whore because I charge for some form of sex, but not a whore in the normal definition of the word; and I'm certainly not an escort because I do not meet my clients. So there we have it: What am I?

I've had callers tell me I should just become a prostitute because I'm basically giving up sex for money anyway. That pisses me off beyond belief. I am nothing like a prostitute, and while I am certainly not putting prostitutes down, I do not sell sex itself—I sell the idea of it.

My husband jokes with me—and I do too—that I'm a phone whore. It's amusing, and while some people would probably find it offensive, I find it hilarious. I'll be taking a call with my husband sitting next to me, and I'll tell the client that I just had sex with two girls. My husband will mouth the word "whore" and give me a dirty look. I have to mute the phone so I can laugh. I think that's really what it's all about: having fun with it. And that's probably why my husband doesn't mind what I do—we constantly joke about it.

What category that suits me best? I'm an actor. I pretend to play with myself; I can become anyone my clients want me to be; I can express any emotion necessary. In fact, I can also do different accents. Qualities like that make for a great actor.

Who Becomes a Phone Sex Operator?

I recently watched an interview on CNN about the rise of housewives becoming phone sex operators because of the economy and below the video, people could post comments. Of course, the first comment was, "People who do this are probably abused as children . . ." And while that could be true, I honestly don't think it is for the most part. It's similar for women who start stripping—mostly because they know they're good looking and men will pay to look at a beautiful woman—basically, it will pay her bills. How many times have you heard of a woman stripping to pay for school? It's because it's "easy" and lucrative. So why are housewives joining the phone sex operator ranks if not for the same reasoning? It's lucrative and easy! And even in this shitty economy, phone sex companies are always hiring because if you don't get a call, it doesn't affect them, they only pay when someone calls you.

I don't believe there is any definitive reason why women start doing phone sex. Me, I just fell into this job. I was never abused or raped. I simply tried it, enjoyed it, and made good money.

What Types of Operators Are There?

Over the years, especially with being a dispatcher, I have heard the real and the fake voices PSOs use and it's quite amusing. I have done a ton of two-girl phone calls and sometimes want to shoot myself with the way a girl is talking to the callers. Other girls, I end up complimenting on how they handled the call. I've ended up defining two different types of phone sex operators : "The Moaner" and "The Realistic."

"The Moaners" are the type of girls who just make moaning sounds during the entire phone call and don't really listen to what the caller says. They feel they need to fill up any and all moments of silence with talk, so they don't stop and probably won't let him get a word in edgewise. These are also the girls who will most likely give their tit size as much bigger then usual, like a 32DD or a 36H, which is usually just unrealistic. I like to keep it somewhat natural and realistic myself.

With some of these girls, even saying "Hi" is drawn out like a moan, with her voice very breathy. The conversation might go this way:

> "Hi, my name is . . . . , ohhh what's yours? Ohh, I like that, mmm, what would you like baby? Yah? Ohh, you mean you want to, ohh, lick my pussy? Ohh, you're such a good boy mmm. Mmmm, I'm sucking your cock baby, (sucking and licking noise). Ohh yah baby, mmm, you like that don't you?"

You get the idea and can understand how annoying that might be . . .

Some guys like these girls, but I am not a moaner. I've been complimented many times on how real I am, and that makes the fantasy all that much better.

So, yes, I categorize myself as "The Realistic"—a girl who listens to the caller and responds accordingly. In the beginning of the conversation, The Realistic will ask the caller personal information to get to know him and make him believe she cares about him and that she's not just doing a job. Some guys hate this because they want to get right to the fantasy, while other guys like to get to know who they are talking to.

However, some of these PSOs get to know their clients well enough and almost consider them friends after they've talked to them for months or years. They will also be able to recognize the caller's voice and remember what they are into and what their previous conversation entailed. So when the client calls back, the PSO and client are able to continue the fantasy or do the same fantasy again—the guy doesn't have to re-explain what he wants.

The conversation might go like this:

> "Hi, I'm . . . . Who's this? So tell me about yourself, baby. What do you like, what are you into? Well, I'm (gives description). Sounds good? So what can I do for you tonight? Would you like to do some role-playing or just pretend that I'm there right now?"

I'm not claiming this is the right character to play, each caller is different and may want one over the other. However, I do believe The Realistic PSO has multiple facets to her character. She is able to change roles easily based on what the client is looking for and it makes the job less taxing. PSOs are actors, as I've said before. They get to play a part in this "play" the guy has written for them, and it can be quite fun.

One way that I, as a realistic PSO, get the client to call back is to make the caller believe I am the person I say I am. I keep the information as close to the truth as possible (with my description and extra curricular activities being similar to my own personality) so I won't forget what I told them later. Granted, if the person asks the dispatcher to give them a certain type of girl, and I don't fit that description, I change the details of my character accordingly. I will keep accurate notes of what I told the caller, so if he calls back and asks for me, I know what I talked about and what I looked like.

The Perks

First and foremost, you're your own boss. Granted, usually you work for a company, but some of them are more lax than others. Some require certain hours in which you must be logged on, and they monitor you pretty strictly, almost like a timecard system. And then there are some that let you have total freedom. Me, I couldn't stand working for companies that had set hours. I mean really? I'm working from home! I don't need to be tied down to certain hours—the point of working from home is the independence to make your own schedule. Second, you can work as much as you want, or as little as you want, depending on how much you want to make.

It's basically a commissioned-based job, so the more calls you take, the more money you make. I've met girls who make $60,000 a year doing this, and I've met girls who only make $5,000 a year. It can be very lucrative if you are good and if you put the time and energy into it.

Third would have to be the occasional free gifts from clients. One of my girls recently got a $250 gift card to Victoria Secret. I have gotten a bicycle, boots, Amazon gift cards and of course, cash. I know one phone sex operator who is really good with financial domination, and she has received plane tickets a few times. Now you're asking, "But wait, don't you have to give out your personal information in order to receive said gifts?" The answer is no. I accept presents through a P.O. Box, and the bike, well, that particular item came about through a caller's Wal-mart gift card. Anything else that can be sent online can be done via e-mail and is totally anonymous. The girl who got the plane tickets? Well, obviously, she had to give out personal information, but that's her prerogative.

Honestly, I only have two clients who know my physical address and five who know my last name and this is out of at least 3000 clients. I have known these clients for seven years and have complete trust in them. It sounds like a "Catch 22", but I judge each person over a long period of time and I never give out my information—aside from my P. O. Box, which has everything addressed as "Box Owner"—to anyone I haven't talked to for at least five years. Not to say I'm recommending that method for everyone; it's just what I do. And as a business owner at this point, I feel I can make that kind of decision safely. For someone just starting out or working for a company, I'd suggest my previous sentiment: never, ever give out your personal information.

The reason I make as much as I do, approximately $60,000 per year, is because I work all the time. And I mean *all* the time. Friends are always asking me, "When do you sleep?" I'll answer the phone any time of the day. I'm a light sleeper, and I figure, why not take a call at night? I can just take a nap later. This is, of course, due in part to the fact that I am a full-time operator, and it's my business. It's my only source of income. Also, I'm very money driven. I like to eat out with my husband and have the extra money to spend on fun things like that, so I have to work hard to make it.

A question I get often is, "How do you find a job like that?" I think the people who ask are really the ones who want to get into it. With the internet, everything is so easy to find. It was odd that I found my first PSO job in a paper, as most can be found online. Usually, it's a random ad, but of course websites dedicated to adult entertainment have job listings as well. Sex sells—this is commonly known. But we never realize just how much it sells until we're making a living off of it. No matter how crappy the economy is, men (especially) always have that little extra cash to play with. When it comes to getting an orgasm, most men will spend that extra cash to talk to a girl to help them get off.

Really, it comes down to this: The fantasy they have, that they like to masturbate to, is something they can't share with their significant others. Therefore, in order to play it out, they have to call and pay for it. That particular fantasy brings on a specific orgasm, especially when it's acted out with a live person. As I've always said, once you orgasm (or cum) to a particular fantasy a few times, your orgasms will not be the same unless you are thinking, acting, or talking about that one fantasy. You're now associating your orgasm with that fantasy. Sometimes it's your best orgasm.

The Downsides

Some of the downsides of this job are also the perks. While you get to work from home and be your own boss, it also means you don't get out and socialize very much. I thought this would be great for me because I'm not very social and am pretty much a homebody anyway. Yet, over the years, I've found myself wishing I could have some form of contact with the outside world, aside from talking about the weather with checkout clerks. When I had a day job, while I was miserable at the actual job, I at least had coworkers to talk to. And while I am on the phone all day long, I will get off the phone with a client and call a friend to chit chat because, of course, the talking done with a client is never the same as chatting with a friend. And when my husband gets home, I'm all mouth and talk his ear off.

Another downside is that it is a commission-based job, which means your paycheck isn't guaranteed. How much you make is directly determined by how many calls you take—by how hard you're willing to work. And sometimes when you're home by yourself, especially every day, the motivation just goes out the window. However, how many calls you take is not only determined by how much you work and how many clients call you, but by simple advertising. Some girls advertise themselves, some work for agencies that do the advertising for them; either way, the calls come in somehow. I've had bad days in which the calls I've taken are all very short, and I don't make much, and then I've had some days where the call lengths are much longer, and I make a nice amount. Personally, I set a quota for myself, usually based off of how much I'd like to make that month, broken into how much I need to make each day—it's a great motivator. I don't stop working that day until I hit that quota.

I also don't have a regular sleep schedule. Sometimes I wake up at 5 a.m. to take a phone call, and I might be up for only 5 minutes. And then I could go back to sleep and be awakened in another 10 minutes—or I may not get a call for another 4 hours. Some of the girls who work for me set themselves schedules, but I feel that limits them.

Some phone sex companies don't make you have a minimum "hold time," and some do. A hold time is how long a PSO has to keep the client on the phone. Some companies are very stringent about that, and you can get fired if you have a low hold time. Some companies will pay more per minute if the hold time is above a certain amount (stipulated by the company). I have only worked for companies with no hold times; they don't care what your hold time is, mostly because the clients are paying for a set amount of time up front. Thus, if you only talk for five minutes, but the client paid for ten, he gets charged ten either way. But you get paid for five, and the company pockets the other five. My own company works the same way. I have a ten minute minimum, so if he talks for only three minutes, he's still charged for ten; therefore, I don't have to deal with hold times. However, I do have a quality guarantee: If a client calls back after three minutes claiming he didn't like the girl, then he doesn't pay.

Downfalls come in all shapes and sizes. One of the worst I've come across is having my true identity discovered. After a couple of years of doing phone sex, I started to use my real name, because using my stage name was a pain in the ass. For instance, I'd be telling a client a story, and then reference myself within the context: "Stacey, why'd you do that . . ." instead of saying Faith. So I gave up and started using my real name. And while my work phone number (the number guys call to talk to me) shows up as my company name, my cell phone does not. And when I went out on my own, I would sometimes return a phone call on my cell phone and forget to block my number. So then some of my clients knew my last name.

Also, my company is a set of initials that are the first letters of the name of an old company I had. Needless to say, I told one of my clients what the letters stood for. So he Googled me. When he found my old website, he saw my name and my real picture. With my real name, he also was able to look me up in the white pages. Granted, nothing came of it aside from him being upset that I lied about what I looked like, and he actually still calls. But who knows what could happen if you're not careful about protecting your identity. I should have known better—I had been doing phone sex for five years at that point.

The only other downfall is when people react poorly when you tell them what you do for a living. I actually haven't had much of a problem telling anyone, and everyone has been relatively receptive to it. However, in the beginning, I did have a hard time telling my family what I did, for fear of how they might react. Yet, when I did tell them, they were supportive and glad that I was happy and doing something that wasn't illegal. So, for me, it wasn't even much of a pitfall with my family. Although I sometimes feel I have to carefully judge each person as to how they might react. The bottom line is, I am proud of what I do, and I have no problem telling people. However, if my father didn't want to tell one of his friends, I'd understand.

Starting On My Own

The first three or four years of my phone sex career, I was only doing it part time, after I got home from my day job. But, like many, I got tired of working for other people and going to a day job that made me miserable. When you don't want to get out of bed every morning, it's time for a career change. I am thankful I had an outletm so many people don't. But I took a huge leap, one I may not have necessarily needed to take right then, but I went for it anyway, I decided to go out on my own, having no idea how I would bring in my own clients.

I had a few clients from other companies I had worked for who started calling me directly (and yes, I technically stole the clients from them, and had them call an 800# I set up. This was very wrong on my part and can't believe I stooped that low back then). I had another website that I sold sexual items on like panties and used dildos and had some clients from there; otherwise, there weren't many. It was hard, but I would go into chatrooms, post ads on Craigslist, and join random adult websites "trolling" for clients. Trolling is a commonly used term in the adult entertainment business. It just means you're looking for clients, seeking them out, to call you. If you've ever been in a chatroom and got instant messaged from a girl (usually), and it looks like a bot (robot), then that is either a girl trolling, or a company who bought a bot to troll for them.

It took some time, but I put together enough clients to pay the bills, with my husband's income supplementing, of course. It was hard for a while because the only way I had for them to pay me was through Paypal, and that worried me because then they'd have my first and last name. Eventually, I made up a business name and opened a Paypal business account instead. I also took some payment prepaid through my P.O. Box and some through Amazon gift cards, it's amazing the lengths men will go to in order to talk to a sexy voice.

I found a website to post an ad for Faith, and the calls started pouring in. I started making more and more, and things got busy. Some of my clients started to ask if I wanted to do a two-girl call with them (invite another girl to chat with us) or if I had another girl he could talk to that was just as good. Through a twist of fate, a client of mine had a girl he wanted to do a two-girl call with. After he was done, this girl, Candace and I started to talk. She needed a job and wanted to take some calls for me. After hiring her, I decided to hire some other girls and put them on the same website I was on that generated all my calls. Again, it was slow going, and I had to do a lot of legwork—and still do!—to keep everything up to date on the girls' sites. But, just like that, so began the start of my own phone sex business.

As I stated before, working as a dispatcher taught me some of the ins and outs of running a phone sex company. I learned ways of keeping track of my clients, their information, and the girls they talked to; some ideas on how to document the girls times; how to answer the phones as a dispatcher, as well as how to deal with the guys who call just to jack off to the dispatcher. I molded my company around the things I liked and didn't like from other companies I had worked for.

For my own business, I'm able to deal with the clients myself as the dispatcher, reassuring them when they ask about the credit card process, girls they want to talk to, etc. Plus, if they call back and say they didn't like the call, I can give them free time, something other companies can't always offer because the dispatcher is just an employee, and therefore, can't authorize any free time. Sometimes being a small company is a good thing. I am able to connect my clients with just the right girl for them. And while it takes up a lot of time doing everything in the company, it saves a lot of money.

CHAPTER FOUR:
The Callers

Over the past seven years of being a phone sex operator, I have talked to thousands of different clients. Some have very unique fantasies while most fall into specific fetishes. From the cross dressing panty boys, ass worshipers, strap-on lovers to the underage, incest and bestiality fantasies.

I've compiled a list of the types of fantasies/fetishes I've encountered, although I'm sure there are many more out there. In my mind, this list is not complete, nor will it ever be complete. The human imagination can encompass so much, and I think sexual fantasies, especially, change and mutate all the time. The most interesting thing is, with each main category of fantasy (for example, enemas) there are numerous different types of fantasies it encompasses. However, this list won't delve into every single fantasy possible; it will simply give you an understanding of the difference between what you once thought phone sex was, and what it really is.

Falling in Love or Wanting to Meet

The most amusing type of guys are the ones who honestly believe you are who you say you are. These are usually the ones who instantly fall in love with you within one phone call and want to meet you or contact you outside of the phone sex realm. Of course, to keep them on the phone longer, you tell them you'll meet them and then make up excuses as to why you can't make it. I will play this game with them for as long as I can, simply because it makes money. If they don't realize this, it's their problem. This may seem dishonest, but it is what it is in the phone sex world. I will drag it out until they honestly seem pissed off that I keep making up excuses. At that point, it's time to give up the game and flat out tell them, "I'm sorry. I have a rule that I do not meet my clients," and leave it at that. Usually, I get an argument from them. At that point, it's repeat as necessary until they understand they aren't going to get anywhere with it.

I have been asked to meet guys more times than I can count. And if I think the guy will become a regular caller, then I'll tell him I will. But if I think he's probably never going to call back again, I'll tell him that I don't meet my clients.

Once, I was told, "I just wanted to let you know that I wasn't using you with this call. I seriously want to be your friend—maybe we can be pen pals." It's laughable. How can you say you're not using me, when you call me specifically to get off? Whether you talk about "making love" or not, you're still calling a phone sex hotline. It's amazing how some of these guys fall into this spell while talking to a girl with a sexy voice. I believe they do this in order to feel better about themselves, to not feel so "dirty" or "low" or "pathetic" for calling a phone sex line. To me, it's a job; to them, it's using someone. We could look at every service industry job that way, if we liked. The girl at the check-out counter. Yeah, we're using her. The guy serving your food? Using him. Doesn't make much sense if you look at it that way. Moving on . . .

Then, of course, there are the guys who, while cumming, will say "I love you," and they want to hear it back. I have no problem telling them I love them if it means they'll be satisfied. It's not like I truly do love them, obviously, but it just so happens to be their specific fantasy. I've had many guys say they really are in love with me and even ask to talk with my mother to try to have her convince me to meet him. There is no end to the ways in which a guy will attempt to meet you.

Forced Feminization

The most common fantasy that I get calls on involves forced feminization. In essence, it isn't really forced because the guy really loves wearing women's lingerie, but he wants to pretend that it's against his will. I guess it makes him feel better about himself—that he has to give into what you say because you are more dominant. It takes the guilt out of it, too; some of the guys are telling themselves they're sick or perverted for wanting to wear women's clothing, or even for wanting to be a woman. So when they get "forced," it's easier to deal with. It's not their fault anymore.

Forced feminization can include anything from making him dress up like a girl to making him take hormones to become a girl. These guys want you to fuck them in the ass, but they want their asses to be called pussies and their cocks to be called clits. They are pretty much becoming transsexuals.

Most of these guys like to be dominated as well as humiliated. They also like to be called names and made fun of for being "sissy faggots" (there is no offense intended here—it's just what they like). What it really boils down to is the humiliation. Some have small dicks and some don't, but either way, in their fantasy, they like to be made fun of, told that their dick isn't big enough and that they could never please a woman. And since their dick is the size of a clit, and since I am dominating them, I'm going to turn them into a girl.

Cock-Sucking Sissy "Faggots"

The word "faggots" may be harsh, but it's actually what these guys like to be called. Basically, if a guy calls me and says he wants to suck a cock but isn't gay, then I berate him for being a "faggot." It makes him feel humiliated and, in turn, want to suck cock more. My theory is that these guys aren't gay but bi, mostly because, in my mind, any respectable gay man doesn't want to be known as a faggot. In fact, a lot of these guys would never go through with actually sucking a cock. It's just the thrill of being "forced," or coerced, into sucking one for a beautiful woman.

Strap-on Play

I have to say that almost every forced feminization and cuckolding roleplay I do involves strap-on play. They always want me to bend them over and use their ass. There are two types of guys who like strap-ons: Ones who want to be used like my little bitch, be fucked until they cum, and really use their ass; and ones who want me to fuck their "pussies" (aka, their asses) and rub their clits (aka, their dicks) while fucking them. The first are guys who are probably executives in whatever company they work for and are constantly telling other people what to do, and they just want to be the one under someone else's control and be submissive to them. The second pretty much want to be girls but not necessarily be put in panties or lingerie. They don't like guys and don't consider themselves gay, but, rather, they consider themselves lesbians.

Underage

I find it fascinating when I talk to guys who are into underage/incest fantasies with their own children and, at the end of the conversation, they'll say they'd never do that to their own kids, nor have they thought about it. Or if they don't have kids, they say that if they did, they'd never even think about it. They claim they know it's wrong and it makes them a sick person, so they would never do it.

My question to them is: "Then why would you fantasize about it in the first place?" None of them have that answer. Granted, I know that is the point of fantasies: to dream of doing something you can't do. But if they had the chance to fulfill their fantasy, would they? If you had a fantasy that you didn't think you could do, then one day was able to without consequence, would you do it? This ties into the sad lack of studies done on people who know they are pedophiles but who refuse to have anything to do with children for fear of hurting a child. These people need help, but they are afraid to ask for it. Sadly, I can tell that I deal with a lot of these people in my line of work, and I wonder if phone sex is their only outlet in this day and age.

Incest

Incest can be just about anything: mother/daughter, father/daughter, brother/sister, mother/son, you get the idea. Freud had it partially right: the most popular incest calls are mother/son and father/daughter. However, the ages range. I've had guys who want me to be their mother and they be the underage ones, and then there are guys who want to be grown up, but me still be their mother. I even have one guy who wants to be in his 20s and to have me (as his mom) yell at him for masturbating when I don't allow it. The mother/son fantasies are almost never forced, but the father/daughter ones are about half-forced and half-willing (meaning that he is forcing his daughter to please him).

Most every guy that I have asked if a parent actually did it to them says no, but that they have always fantasized about it. I have also had guys say they like doing the mother/son fantasies, but they don't like to think about it being their actual mother, just a pretend one.

Bestiality

Bestiality calls are just thrilling! Can you sense the sarcasm? Because like it's actually fun to talk about fucking my dog or horse. It's pretty straight forward, but I still get asked by non-PSOs what callers want me to do to an animal. Basically, they want me to talk about sucking off and getting fucked by a dog, for the most part. I do have a client who loves hearing about my adventures to a local barn and sucking on and/or trying to fuck a horse. This is the one fantasy I have a lot of trouble with still. It's so gross to me because I care about animals very much. It takes a lot to ignore how disturbing it is and to avoid picturing it in your mind.

Cuckolding

A big fantasy for some men is to watch their women get fucked—this is called a cuckold fantasy. These guys want to watch you with a guy with a much bigger cock than their own. I always have them sit in the corner in a chair, or sit on the edge of the bed right next to me, and stroke their dick while I fuck someone else, explaining to them how I'm looking directly at them as I'm sucking or fucking this other guy. Or, sometimes they like to have their dick compared side by side to the guy you're fucking. They want you to show them how much bigger this guy is.

Most guys will also either want to lick your ass or pussy while you're being fucked. Sometimes they'll want to suck the guy's cock to taste your juices off of them, but most of the time they will want to eat you out after the cum is inside of you. Although they say they aren't gay, what would you call wanting to eat a man's cum out of a girls' pussy?

The next extreme to the cuckold fantasy is when a client wants to watch their significant other get gang banged. The point of this is the guys feel they are so insignificant that their significant other needs all those cocks at once in order to please her. The reality is, that's more of what will turn the caller on, than what would turn his significant on.

Stocking/Pantyhose Fetishes

A lot of pantyhose fetishes involve the men actually wearing pantyhose or stockings themselves. I didn't know the difference between pantyhose and stockings until a few years after I started doing phone sex. In fact, I have one client who has more knowledge of stockings and pantyhose than anyone I've ever known. There are so many different brands of pantyhose out there. Man, I must be slumming it because one of the guys actually buys $40 pairs of pantyhose.

The other types I deal with involving pantyhose are the ones who like to be teased with a woman who's wearing them. One client likes to be touched with pantyhose and even tickled; the other wants to be spanked while over the knees of a woman wearing pantyhose. All these fantasies happen because of something that happened in their childhood, which is actually what I've been told by the clients themselves.

ABDL—Adult Baby/Diaper Lover

Adult babies are by far my favorite callers. They are so sweet and innocent. They want to pretend to be a baby and just be coddled, pampered, and really loved. They want to be held and have their diaper changed and even drink milk from your breasts. You get to talk to them like you would a small child, talk about how you'd change them, sometimes punish them by spanking them, all the things you might do to a child. Sometimes they do want to be played with sexually, but 80 percent of the time they don't. The one thing to keep mind is that I'm not talking to them as if I am molesting a child; I'm talking to them as if I'm talking to a grown man who wants to be a baby. There is a very thin line between it. I've even had a guy who wanted me to sing nursery rhymes to him until he fell asleep on the phone.

Ass Worship

Ass worship is very common and usually involves "tossing the salad"—i.e., eating out the PSO's ass. Some guys don't want to eat your ass when it's dirty, while others want to know how much exercise you've done that day and how sweaty it is for them to clean up—or even more dirty than that. It's hard to know exactly what the guy wants, but most of them will usually tell you. I start out by having them "clean" my ass crack, and if they ask, "Is it dirty Mistress?" then that means they want it dirty. So I simply tell them it is, and then they're "forced" to clean it. I usually start with my crack, either by bending over, or by smothering them by sitting on their face. They will then work their way in—they aren't just cleaning me; they're pleasing me as well. When I have a guy who wants to be my bitch and worship my ass, I very rarely let him touch me in any other way, nor will I let him lick or touch my pussy. I usually tell them they aren't privileged enough for my "sweet pussy."

Foot Worship

As weird as this may sound, foot worship ties into ass worshipping. Sometimes, when I have a caller who's a sissy and wants to be my bitch, I'll start him out by kissing my boots, then my feet, and then sucking on my toes. Sometimes guys like smelly feet, and I'll have him lick my feet clean and be very descriptive about it. I usually make a guy spend quite some time on my feet before he'll be allowed to worship my ass. And on the flip side, some guys don't want anything but your feet. I will also make these guys my footstools: they have to get on all fours when I want to relax and watch TV, and I put my feet on their back. They also should beg to worship their Mistress's feet.

Boot/Shoe Worship

What I like to do with boot fetishes is to force the guy to sit in front of my closet and clean all my boots with his tongue. I berate him and tell him he's not worthy enough of anything else. A lot of boot, shoe, or foot fetishes involve the guy feeling he's not worthy enough for the girl's pussy, so he starts with the feet, until he is worthy. A lot of the Mistress calls I do involve the guy starting by licking my boots. But I do have guys who just love feet and want to have them rubbed all over their bodies or just want to suck on them. I don't know about you, but I don't like to have my toes sucked on. However, I have a friend who loves it.

Panty Smelling

This one is pretty straight forward as well. The callers usually want to talk about me sitting on their faces and the smell of my pussy and ass through my panties—or I take them off and put them on their face. Usually they aren't very extreme, but I have one client who likes to take it a little far. Robby D likes me to talk about how I went No. 2 in my panties while at work. When I get home, I take them off and throw them at him. He likes me to force him to smell, taste, and clean them. I have to be very descriptive about the brown color, the shitty smell, etc.

Toilet Training

This isn't what you're thinking. It has nothing to do with teaching them how to go to the bathroom. Instead, it involves teaching them how to drink pee or poop (depending on which they're into), straight from a woman's body. I talk in detail about how I will make them drink my pee, or I talk about pissing over their face. Just like most of the fantasies I deal with, it involves complete humiliation and degradation.

Somewhat similar to toilet training are toilet boys. These guys like to worship your ass and be used as your toilet paper. You no longer need a toilet bowl or toilet paper because you've now got his mouth and tongue. He will be at your beck and call, and be ready and available for you to piss or shit in his mouth when you need to. And he has to make sure you are perfectly clean and that he doesn't spill a drop, or he'll be punished. With these guys, I always tell them they will be my live-in slave and sleep either at the end of the bed on the floor or at my feet. That way, I tell them, if I have to go to the bathroom in the middle of the night, I can just kick them to wake them up.

Pee Men

These guys want to hear you pee. I have a guy who calls me a few times a week in the morning because he knows it's a guarantee that if he wakes me up, I'll have to pee.

Enemas

These calls go hand-in-hand with toilet boys, or guys who want to be used as your toilet. With enemas, there are two different fantasies that I've come across. The first involves the PSO having an enema, and the guy telling you how to hold in the water and exactly how to do it. This usually ends in one of two ways: releasing the enema and cumming for him, or releasing the enema water into his mouth.

The second version of this fantasy is where the caller wants the PSO to give him the enema. He likes to lose control, be told how much water to pump inside of his ass and how long to hold it for. Usually, I tell him to plug up his ass with a butt plug after he fills it, and then sit on the butt plug until I tell him to take it out. Once he's ready to release the water, he's either going to release it in the bathtub or toilet, or somehow get the water to his mouth. Usually he cums after releasing it.

CBT—Cock and Ball Torture

I'll talk more about other forms of torture guys want to receive. But with CBT, I have seen and heard some crazy shit. Sometimes, my husband will have to leave the room because just hearing it makes his dick hurt. Russ D. performs on cam for one of my other PSOs. I've watched him on cam myself, and it's pretty messed up. He likes to have his balls tied up and his dick usually locked in chastity. When he is allowed to have his cock released from chastity, he is told to slap his balls, his cock, put knitting needles down his peehole, rub his cock with hot sauce or sandpaper and even sew up his peehole . . . the list goes on and on. You name it, and he'll do it for his Mistress.

Tease and Denial and Guided Masturbation

Tease and denial usually goes along with guided masturbation. Starts out with guided masturbation, in which I tell them exactly how to stroke their dicks, down to every last detail. Then I make them get really excited and tell them to stop stroking. I keep doing it over and over again until I'm ready to let them cum. It's actually quite fun, but sometimes a little tedious, however, it's a great way to extent out your call!

Rape and Torture

This might sound weird, but sometimes I laugh at the rape calls. The reason: These guys want to force you to suck their cock. If a guy was going to rape me, but first force me to suck his cock, I'd bite it off! I don't think I've actually heard of a rape that involved a guy forcing a woman to suck his cock.

Rape is about control—getting the act done with as fast as possible. These callers most likely have never actually raped a woman, nor do they actually plan on doing it. Therefore, I don't find these calls as offensive as

I probably could. The thing I hate to do is make the noises as if I'm being raped, it can be really upsetting.

Then there are the guys who call and want to talk about how I would hire guys to rape their wife. With this fantasy, it is my opinion these men have some sort of animosity toward their wives or girlfriends and want to see them harmed.

The torture calls really suck because you not only have to scream and cry as if you're being tortured, but you also have to give detailed descriptions of what they are doing to you. Sometimes I feel really sick to my stomach describing how a guy is cutting me, etc. Sometimes the calls get a little out there, similar to the torture scenario with Larry, but sadly to say, since him, I've had worse.

And to be honest, I rarely do these calls anymore; I'd rather hang up and lose the money then discuss raping someone.

Torture to the Guy Calling

You're probably thinking this is going to be like CBT. And while it does involve some torture of the client's dick, it also involves torture of every other body part.

One of my clients, Carl L., loves being tortured. He usually spends about $300 a week calling me and my other girls. Carl usually calls us while he's drunk and wants us to tell him about all the crazy stuff we would do to him, such as cutting off his tongue, grilling his fingers, making him eat our pee and poop, forcing him to eat dog poop, making him drink bleach. And he just wants to hear it over and over again, no matter how repetitive it is. It's amusing to come up with new and interesting tortures for him—sadistic, but it's harmless entertainment.

Baby Sitters

There are so many different types of baby sitter fantasies. There's the obvious one—which I'm sure every married man with kids fantasizes about—in which he drives the babysitter home and she comes onto him. Then there's the one where the babysitter has sex with the child. Or the one where the babysitter brings her boyfriend over to play with the child. Or the one that goes along with guys who are sissies (in my opinion), and the father comes home early to catch the babysitter getting fucked and then eats the boyfriend's cum out of her afterward. Again, the human imagination is limitless.

Daddy's Little Girl

This involves the guy who wants to pamper you (as if you were a little girl) and then have his way with you. Amazingly enough, a lot of these calls don't involve rape, but a willing participant. Essentially, they want their daughters, no matter how old, to actually want to be with their fathers in a sexual manner.

BBW—Big Beautiful Women

This seems to be a new thing. Some men are just turned on by larger women, and others feel humiliated by eating a larger girl out or having her sit on their face. I'm not sure why there seems to be a sudden jump in these types of callers, maybe because the obesity rate is rising, or maybe because, from my experience—the majority of PSOs are large themselves and have been using their own picture, instead of a model's picture.

Gynecological Exams

For a while, with one of the companies I worked for, this was a somewhat common fantasy. This is the guy who wants to give you a gynecological examination, or wants you to give it to other girls, usually younger ones. You have to go into detail about what you'd do to each girl. Let me tell you, I had no idea what a speculum was before I had one of these calls! And you know how hard it is to describe what you'd do to the girls? I have no idea what my OBGYN does when she examines me. So, of course, I had to do some research for this one. Usually it's pretty straight forward: talking about spreading open the vagina, although you usually call it a pussy (rarely do guys every want you to call it a vagina), and the girl is in just a little bit of pain. Of course, they want you to play with the girls and make them cum too. How more unrealistic could this be!?

One of my first callers involving OBGYN exams wanted me to be in a Sorority and that each pledge had to go through a gynecological exam as part of the hazing. It wasn't anything painful—just a bunch of girls, naked, in the basement, giving one another gyno exams.

Pimps

These are the guys who would prostitute out their own wives, or as one liked to fantasize about, getting a mail-order bride just to whore her out. They really think they are hot shit, and they're the best women can get, and therefore, they can do whatever they want to their women. Ultimately, they really can't, which is why they're calling a sex line. It's like a man getting a large car or something to over compensate for as mall dick.

Sound Effect Men

These are the guys who make sounds like they are licking or sucking on you. Sometimes, I have to mute the phone to laugh because the sounds they make aren't very realistic or a turn-on for me. Better yet, I've never heard a guy make those types of noises in the bed room. That's probably what makes it even funnier. Let me have you try it: Stick out your tongue and make a blah-blah-blah noise. Does that sound sexy?

Advice Seekers

These are sad cases. They call to talk, not to have phone sex. I literally played psychiatrist to Matt, who said he was constantly depressed and almost suicidal. We talked a couple times, and I felt so bad for him that I eventually found a name of an actual psychiatrist in his area. He sends me an e-mail from time to time letting me know he's okay and what's new in his life. If I haven't heard from him in a couple of months, I send him the e-mail instead, checking up on him. Thankfully, it's been about five years, and we are still in touch. He never calls to have phone sex with me; he just e-mails me and says "I'm still alive. How are you?" It's not that these people don't have friends or family. I'm sure they do. However, it's sometimes much easier to talk to a complete stranger than to someone you're close to about something this personal.

Super-Heroine Fantasies and Shrinking/Growing Fantasies

These are quite interesting, and I feel like I'm very good at them because they involve a lot of on-the-spot imagination. I have a caller who is a guy, also a phone sex operator, and does these calls as a "woman" with other men. He calls me to do them with me, too, and narrates them for me, so that he can masturbate to them. (He pretends to be a girl when he talks to other guys as a PSO). I actually enjoy the calls because he's amazingly good at detail and has helped me out tremendously; in fact, these types of fantasy calls are all he does with his other clients.

Basically the concept is that the girl is a superhero, disguised as a secretary or babysitter or whatever he wants, and he discovers it, but she takes control of him because she's so much stronger than he is. It really has to do with strength, power, and control.

This goes hand in hand with the shrinking and growing fantasies. In these fantasies, the guy shrinks and the woman grows, making the guy feel submissive and powerless. I've actually had guys want me to shrink them down so much that they are dildo-sized, and then I use them to fuck myself. Once of my clients wants me to be a scientist and I develop a pill, that when taken, makes the men shrink and the woman grow. He doesn't want to be shrunk down to midget size, but just a foot or 2 smaller than the woman, making her almost Amazon-like.

Celebrity Impersonation

These are quite amusing, and I usually end up laughing afterward. I've played Jessica Alba, Miley Cyrus, and Demi Moore, to name a few. I've also played characters from Grey's Anatomy, Bones, CSI, and Sex in the City. The fantasies themselves are usually not kinky at all—they just want me to be her. Although I don't sound like any of the celebrities I portray, and I don't even try to change my voice because I'm far from an impersonator. One caller, Charlie, would have me pick my favorite TV show and he would play a character from it, and I would play the female counterpart. It was straight sex—we just used the names of the characters. Then he started to write his own scripts about pirates, fairies, and princesses, and I would read them out loud to him.

Drug Fantasies

I can't say this is exactly a fantasy or not. Really, it's just the guy doing drugs on the other end. A lot of these guys can't say exactly what they are doing. The calls aren't monitored, but they find it hard to say they are snorting coke. They'd prefer to say that they are "powdering their nose." And I retort, "just say you're snorting coke!" Their line to me is always "What if the government is listening in?" Come on, do you really think the government cares if you're talking about doing drugs while on a phone sex hotline? Whippets are very popular lately. Guys do those like crazy when they talk to me!

Blackmail

Queer boy, (yes, he has me call him Queer Boy) is another cock sucking "faggot" who likes to be teased about being gay, however he also likes blackmail. The fear of me posting the pictures he's taken of him sucking cock, him in lingerie, or of his small dick, up on the internet or emailing them to people he knows, turns him on. In fact, on occasion, when he pisses me off, I will post them for awhile! We have developed a website that is hisname.com.

I have all his personal information, his social security number, his address, his work address, his wife's work address, his sister-in-law's name and number, and I've even run a background check on him (with him paying of course) to make sure everything checked out. It's the constant threat of being "outed" that gets him going, as it is for most blackmail fantasies.

Racism

It may sound weird and pretty wrong, but I actually get guys who want to be yelled at and made fun of for their race. I have had people who are Jewish, African American, and Asian who have asked me to go off on them racially. I mean they want me to use every slang term in the book—without going into the details of which—and just yell at them, calling them pathetic and worthless and so on.

I am choosing to not go into any details of what I said; except for with Josh and Tyrone, both were black men who called me who wanted to be racially humiliated by me. So I made both jump around and make monkey noises—calling them porch monkeys, eat watermelon out of my ass, fart on their fried chicken, etc. Josh even wanted me to tell him black jokes—which of course I knew none—so I had to go to Wikipedia.com and search for "black jokes" to read to him!

It's insane to me that someone would want that, but to each their own.

CHAPTER FIVE:
Bring Out the Freaks

Throughout the years I have heard some pretty crazy fantasies, from either guys who have called me or from the dispatchers or operators from the agencies I've worked for. I've added some of the more interesting (for lack of a better word) ones in this section.

There is no particular order to their freakishness.

On the Lighter Side

The ABC Guy

Jeremy wanted to play the Alphabet game with me. He wanted me to say a letter, starting with A, give a word associated with sex starting with that letter, and then use it in a sentence. Here is what I came up with:

A—Anal—I can't wait to have anal sex with you tonight.
B—Balls—I love playing with your balls in my mouth.
C—Cunt—I need your cock in my cunt now!
D—Dick—Your dick feels so good in my mouth.
E—Eat—You feel so good when you eat my pussy.

You get the idea.

Pedal Pumping

I've only dealt with one guy who was into this, but I did look it up later to learn more. He sent me this video of a close up of a woman's foot in high heels on a pedal of an older car, the ones with the big, fat gas pedal. And it's the sound of the revving of the engine along with looking at the woman's foot in high heels that gets him off. It's called Pedal Pumping. Nowadays, it's a woman pumping on any car's pedal, but for him, it was the old style pedals that he enjoyed, because it brought him back to his childhood. He said he could remember how his hot, older next door neighbor would rev the engine of her old car in her driveway, and he would watch from his window.

Cactus Man

What would someone want to do with a cactus?! The caller wanted me to pretend I was a horse and he was a cactus. And he wanted me to eat him. He asked me to make sounds like I was eating: "Yum, yum, yum. I'm a horse, and I'm eating you, the cactus . . . yum, yum, yum." Etc. Try and do that call with a straight face!

Ironing Board?

One day, I took a call, and the guy asked me how kinky I could get. I'm imagining a sick, twisted fantasy, prepping myself, and I said, "Anything you want." He asked me if I had an ironing board and an iron, and to tell him what brand it was. I don't own an iron and have no idea what the brand names are, so I told him it was an old iron that my mom gave me when she bought a new one (which was good because he ended up really liking that). He then asked if I had a silk nightie and to tell him what the tag said. I didn't have a silk nightie either, so I made something up and said 80 percent silk and 20 percent polyester. He then guided me through what he wanted: "Turn the iron to a regular setting and start ironing the silk nightie." I told him in detail exactly how I was ironing it.

After a few minutes of me describing the fabric getting warm and the wrinkles coming out, he asked me, "How badly do you want me to cum?" Of course, I said, "Very badly, baby." So he said, "Then turn the iron all the way up." I responded, "But then I'll burn it," and his response back was "Oh, yeah!" And so I told him exactly how I was burning my silk nightie—how it was turning black and curling up under the heat. And amazingly enough, he got off to that. At the end of the call, I had to ask him if he knew where the fantasy had come from. He said he had no idea, but that it had to be something from his childhood.

Teddy Bears

There is a fetish group in which the members call themselves fluffies. These people dress up in costumes that look like mascots or giant stuffed animals, and they play with one another sexually. However, to put a spin on it, one caller wanted to talk about how he was rubbing teddy bears against his cock. He loved to hump and rub against teddy bears to get off. I told him he should cut a hole in one so he could fuck it. Nothing came of it, unfortunately, because that would have been hilarious!

Sound Effects

Henry wanted me to make fart sounds. He wanted me to put my tongue between my lips and blow. He said to do it over and over until he came. I said nothing for five straight minutes—I just made the sounds. At the end of the conversation, he said, "You have a great night. God bless you and don't let anyone hurt you." I had no response to that one, it was certainly a first.

Then there's the guy who wanted me to sneeze over and over again. It was difficult because the first time he called me, I ran around the house, looking for dust, putting the cats in my face, anything to make myself sneeze. But I couldn't! Finally, he told me to pretend. The few times he called back, I continued faking the sneezes. He didn't want me to say anything, just sneeze; in fact, when I talked too much, he'd end the call. It became obvious the sound of sneezing alone, not the situation in which I was sneezing, was what got him going.

And then there's the guy who used to call and ask me to blow my nose really hard into the phone. Sometimes that's difficult, too, because if your nose doesn't need to be blown, it just plain sucks. Other days, he calls at just the right time. I've told him I won't do it anymore, though, because my nose hurts too much after five minutes of blowing.

Fur

A caller who's fantasy has stayed with me the most is a guy I call the "Fur Coat Man." I haven't talked to him since the first company I worked for, seven years ago, but I still remember what he wanted in every detail. In the beginning of the conversation he wanted me to tell him how much I loved his "nigga cock." (Yes, said just like that. You'd be surprised at how many black men I talk to like to be called "nigger.") He wanted me to be fat and like brown showers (i.e., being shit on). He gave me really weird names like Carol Massive Nose McClusky. He told me to hold my nose so I would sound nasaly, or he'd ask me to say Chris Ridgedface Reckshire in a Russian accent. Other names were: Brit Big Nose Whiner (with a New York accent), Gina Gravel Face Gregarious, and Gina Diarrhea Sniffer DiGluglimo.

He loved it when I said things in a New York/Jewish accent and acted snooty. Throughout the call, he would talk about ass sniffing or choking on his cock. He had a thing for noses—he made me talk about them all the time and liked me to snort like a pig.

He also had a thing with his ass. The icing on the cake was his fantasy of shitting on a white fur coat and rubbing said shit covered coat all over his ass. Hence, he will forever be known as the "Fur Coat Man."

Ironically enough, he is not the only guy I've talked to who was into fur; there are other guys who like to jack off with a fur coat or just a piece of fur. Most like the descriptions of the type of fur, the feel, the color, etc.

Pantyhose Fetishes

I talk to guys who have major pantyhose fetishes all the time. One is Pantyhose Girl (the name he/she goes by). He calls himself a sissy girl, but, really, all he likes is pantyhose, nothing else feminine. He certainly takes it to the extreme, though. When he calls, he talks about how much he likes pantyhose itself, all the different brands, and how much I like them (yes, I pretend to love pantyhose as much as he does to keep him happy). He wants to be called pathetic for his obsession with pantyhose. We talk about how he wants to touch my pantyhose or his all day long. He knows so much more about pantyhose than I do. He ought to sell them for a living.

He goes on cam sometimes, rubbing his feet together with his pantyhose on. But—and here's where he's different from any other pantyhose lover I've met—he buys a larger pair in which he cuts a hole for his head and then puts his arms through the legs. He'll put another pair on his legs as well, so that his whole body is covered in pantyhose. It's like something you'd see in a bizarre Vegas show—amusing and interesting.

Accents and Voices

As wrong as it is, sometimes I can't help but laugh at some of the accents I hear, or even the ones I'm asked to do.

One of the funniest callers with an "accent" sounded like Forrest Gump. Imagine trying to not crack up laughing if Forest said "Jenny, cum in my mother fucking mouth!" Of course, the idea is completely wrong.

Another caller was a sweet old man who had a very bad stutter—he was one of my favorites. He said he was 86 years old, loved to eat pussy, but had never had an orgasm. He rambled a lot, but was so sweet sounding that I just felt bad for him. I don't think the stutter or never having an orgasm was part of a fantasy—he was that sincere.

The whisperer was another sweet caller. I could barely hear him—I'd joke that he must be jacking off in a closet, and that's why he had to be so quiet. Later, the dispatcher told me that he had a tracheotomy, which made me feel horrible about laughing about him. Needless to say, after I learned that, I was much more understanding and sensitive when I asked, "What did you say, hon?"

Psychics

Another company I worked for required the callers to purchase blocks of time, and Eddy would buy hour-long blocks of time each session—and then most often add on more time as the call went on. He thought he was psychic—he'd tell me things about myself that usually weren't correct: my birthday, the number of times I'd had sex, etc. I'd react with shock and amazement and tell him how eerie it was that he knew so much about me. In reality, he was only right three times, probably because he had guessed so many times he was bound to get something right.

Eventually, he became determined to meet me. He tried and tried to convince me that because he knew so much about me, it was okay that we met. I kept telling him I wasn't sure, just to drag it out, get him calling back. Needless to say, that lie dragged it out for about a week. He was so delusional that he thought we knew each other in a past life.

We got to the point where I couldn't keep stretching out the "I'm not ready yet" line. I can usually keep up a charade like that for months, but because we were talking for such long stretches at a time, the two weeks I was in communication with him seemed much longer. Eddy wanted to talk to my mother to share his intentions and to convince her it was safe for us to meet. I got desperate and asked a my mother-in-law to help out and pretend to be my mother. I told Eddy that he wasn't allowed to talk sexual to my "mother," or I'd hang up and never talk to him again. My "mother" pretended to be interested in Eddy, but by the end of the conversation, she forbade me to meet him and said we needed to get to know each other more. All of that we had came up with to tell him, in hopes he'd give up on asking to meet me for awhile longer.

That convinced him to push it out another week, but ultimately, he was more desperate to meet me than I was to keep him as a client. Eddy started to get angry, saying I was toying with him and would actually never meet him. Finally, I had to admit that I had made up my mind, and my "new" rule was I wouldn't meet my clients. That did it for dear old Eddy. He didn't want to talk to me anymore.

Steve, whom I mention in the questions section, was the opposite of Eddy—he thought I was the psychic one. I have to wonder who calls a phone sex line looking for a psychic, but he is very sincere; he truly believes I can predict things. Steve has been my client for seven years now and asks the same questions over and over again.

His "fantasy" involves asking me questions about this woman he met 15 years ago. He wants to know how her tits and pussy look after the sex and partying she has done, or if her pussy was stretched after having kids. He asks who she iss fucking, how big he iss, etc.—all of these questions, over and over and over again.

He has given up enough information about himself and the girl he wants to know about (again, see the questions section), that I have been able to look her up on places like MySpace and Facebook. Needless to say, it was easy to guess what she looks like based off of her pictures. Or sometimes I'd say something like "I see her at a club, with two of her girlfriends, and she's wearing a green top," all based off of a picture on her online social profile.

I'm very surprised he never caught on to that gimmick. Or maybe he did and just didn't care.

Just Plain Weird

When I worked as a dispatcher for the first company (I've worked for several since), I was told many times about a caller some of the other PSOs had dealt with. What he wanted was to talk about women with hairy arms wearing really elegant watches. He liked to talk about how the long arm hair protruded through the wristbands, which had to be gold. There was nothing sexual ever said. I eventually did talk to this guy as an operator myself, and nothing sexual was ever uttered, but he got off regardless.

Somewhat along the same lines: I spoke to one man only once who wanted me to be a girl with thick, black glasses and to talk about the glasses and how they looked on my face.

One of my PSO friends who has been in the business for over a decade still remembers the caller who wanted to put a mouse inside of her so he could send his snake up to get it—a real mouse, and a real snake.

Another caller wanted me to squat over a mirror and describe my ass hole. What makes a perfect ass hole, I'll never know. Ironically, another caller requested I describe my pussy while over a mirror. You really have to learn to bullshit these guys.

Fred was super weird and this is the email he sent me: *I have a request for a story, would roleplay with me where you are a giantess and you use me as a human dildo, the problem is you don't let me out, your hungry pussy ends up melting its victims never to release them. Could you talk about you wet tight pussy sucking me into your stinky trap. could you use the word "trap" as often as possible and really explain from my standpoint what its like trapped in the insides in your tight sticky walls.*

A lot of guys have "key words"—words or phrases that really get them going. Fred's was "trap," another really liked "fuck," and others have been more detailed. I wonder at what point did those specific words become such a driving force for these men's fantasies?

Guy wore a scuba outfit, with a pink leotard and tights under it outfit. He wanted me to tell him I was going to make him a scuba diver, and put on a mask on with laughing gas going into it. He wanted me to tell him I was going to gas him to turn him into a woman. And, he actually said he was wearing the outfit he described, including the mask and was inhaling laughing gas as we talked, although, he didn't laugh . . . hmm.

Then there was another guy who wanted me to role-play that I was a salesman who came and tried to sell him satin sheets. And then of course, he wanted to try them out, so we made his bed up and fucked on the sheets.

On the Sicker Side (although, it depends on what you view as being sick):

It was very hard to categorize these, because they are so out there that there aren't many people with similar fantasies like theirs that I've come across.

Children (skip if offended by this topic, just stating facts)

There was a sick guy I thankfully only had to talk to once, and it was a short phone call. He would tell me how he liked to fuck one year olds and kill them with his big cock.

———————————

There was a guy who wanted to torture little Nazi girls.

———————————

Then of course right after 911 we got a lot of calls from guys wanting to torture little Iraqi girls.

———————————

One guy didn't say anything after he described his fantasy to me, then he made me talk about it in detail. He wanted me to tell him how'd he'd rape and kill a girl, then continue to fuck her after she was dead.

———————————

I talked earlier about Larry, who made me think about quitting. Another caller, whose name escapes me, made me start to question it again, years down the line. He called and told me that he and his wife had an autistic child and they would drug and rape her. Besides the child being autistic that they were raping, which you would think was disturbing enough, his wife would read scriptures out of the bible while he did things to his daughter. Luckily I only had to talk to him once as well.

Magical and Fantasy

Magical and fantasy roleplays are rare. When I say fantasy, I don't mean a generic fantasy, I mean something along the lines of Avatar. When I say magical, I mean roleplaying like I'm a witch.

My favorite magical fantasy was when I got to become a "Sexy Witch," per this client. So I guess we can refer to him as Sexy Witch Man. Here is the email he sent to me, describing his first fantasy he wanted me to do with him. After that, we would change a few of the details, but the majority of it stayed the same.

He wrote: *"Let me tell you a little about my Bewitching fantasy. We are together at my place and after some hot kissing you tell me you have a secret and want to show me. I say ok shot and you start to tell me the story.*

Well I bought these shoe from an old lady (They are pink 4 and a half inch wedge heel shoes) who told me that they are very special, but instead of trying to explain it, I'll show you.' I see you stand up and rub your heels together, they start to sparkle and glow as you slowly put your hand in the air then you put them down to your sides and turn your palms up (they begin to glow as well) then you start chanting (i.e. speaking in tongue or incantation) to call upon your Magical Powers.

I start to feel wind blowing around me as your sexy hair turns jet Black and grows down your back half way then stops and curls ups at the end.

Then you purse your lips and ruby red lipstick appear on your lips. Then your fingernail (still Glowing) begin to grow two inches long and ruby red fingernail polish appears on then.

I see your breast begin to grow bigger to a perfectly round 34Cs. Then your ass and hips become a little bigger, curvy and sexy.

Then sheer black pantyhose appear on your lovely legs. Then your sexy pink 4 and a half inch wedge heel sandal (still Glowing) morph into black sexy 5 and a half inch stiletto ankle strap pumps.

Then your whole body begins to spark and glow even brighter and your sexy pink dress morphs into a very sexy Elvira like dress with slits on both sides going up to your hip for easy access on your body.

You cast a spell (speaking in tongue) and make us both hot and horny for each other. We start to kiss then you see my dick and grab it and say "this dick is not big enough for me" so you cast a spell (speaking in tongue) on it and I then hear you say repeatedly "Grow" and it gets bigger, longer, wider then you suck on it long and hard.

Then you get on top of me and put that big long dick you just made in your pussy and ride it slow fast and hard. And as your riding my big dick you cast a powerful cum spell (speaking in tongue) and take control of my dick as I hear you say out loud "CUM" and it makes me cum like a fountain in you and you cum as well.

I don't know why but High Heels and Sexy Witches are a very big turn on to me. I think it was just too much BeWitched when I was little and it's been a turn on."

The first time we talked I read the email back to him, just changing things as I went as if I was explaining what was happening, instead of him telling me. I would get emails from him when he was ready to play again saying things like, "my sexy witch, are you ready to play again? But this time, will you morph into Beyonce?" I morphed into Jennifer Lopez, Beyonce, and Mariah Carrey. I think he had a thing with woman with big butts!

Now when it comes to a fantasy roleplay, this caller takes the cake. Here is the email he wrote me about what he wanted: *"You're basically an invincible assault machine. Unnatural strength, unnatural speed and agility. You can extend claws from your fingertips, you can open firecanals at the back of your throat and breathe fire, the amount of destruction depending on how many firecanals you've opened (1-4 where 1 = playful and 4 = a nuclear detonation). Your tongue is unnaturally long, and you can lash out with it to capture victims.*

Finally, you can extend a long row of spikes from between your breasts, down between your legs, up your back and coming full circle as it runs over your head. These spikes you can move at great speed, turning yourself into a walking sawblade. You orgasm from killing, you only take girls, and you never deny yourself any pleasures, no matter what."

Unfortunately, or well fortunately, I'm not sure which, he never did end up calling me. I would have loved to have done this fantasy with him, only to find out where else he would have liked to have taken it. The first half of it would have been somewhat fine, until he talked about killing girls and orgasming from it, that's where it turned even weirder (like you thought that was possible!). I would have at least liked to ask where he got the fantasy from and what about it turned him on. However, in my experience, it was the last sentence that explains exactly what did it for him. It was the fact that me as this "invincible assault machine" liked to kill girls to make myself orgasm. It is my opinion, based on my experience, that it was the killing of the girls, which I assume he'd want a detailed explanation of, that made him climax.

Luke called me one afternoon and tells me to imagine that I'm in the library, and I find a book, with an old leather cover, covered in dust. And when I open the book and start to read it, it pulls me into it and become one of the characters, not realizing I'm in the book, it's as if nothing happens. And of course, Luke is narrating the story for me.

He starts out with Chapter 1, where I am in a house, doing the dishes, it's a beautiful day out and I am looking out the window at the green grass. It being a gorgeous day out, I decide to go out and bring a blanket, lay it on the ground. After laying down on the blanket, feeling the breeze flow through my hair, and soaking up the rays of the sun, kissing my body all over, I decide to *enjoy* the sun more and get naked.

He then goes on to talk about letting the rays of the sun touch a part of my body that it has never touched before. I roll over and get on all fours, with my face in the blanket, I reach back and spread my butt cheeks and I feel the sunshine on my butthole—my "rosebud" (which is a common name guys I talk to use for the butthole).

He read me chapter by chapter of this book he came up with, being very explicit and detailed about the sex scenes, and discussing ALL taboos!

It was quite interesting and inventive actually.

Another inventive fantasy was where I'm a super heroine whose body is impenetrable. I fly naked because I fly so fast that my clothing rips right off as I fly. And since I am invincible, I am not afraid of anyone seeing me naked.

When I come across an assailant, I might take their .44 magnum (his choice of gun) and push it inside my pussy and force him to pull the trigger, having the bullets fly inside of me, bounce around and give me orgasms. I also take grenades and put them up inside of me and explode them for the vibrations as well. And of course, man's most dangerous weapon, the nuke, is my play toy. I straddle it and ride it and orgasm from the fun, thrill and of course, the power between my legs, and then I fly and play in the mushroom cloud. And when I scream from an orgasm, it's like a sonic boom, blowing out windows and destroying buildings.

Wanting to Die

Who would think that a guy would want to talk about being killed and masturbate to it! I know there are tons of people who are into asphyxiation as a means of masturbation, but being killed?

One of these callers I've talked to wanted to be electrocuted in his electric chair he said he bought. (I would love to know if he actually had one like he said) He would have me explain exactly how he would die, all the details (which I will spare here), about how it would look, sound and even smell while he was being electrocuted.

A caller who would lead the whole story about how I was his girlfriend's friend and who was an avid gym goer. My boyfriend was a karate instructor and taught me a lot and I, in turn, was teaching his girlfriend. The reason for me to teach her was so that she could control, beat up and abuse her boyfriend. The torture involved lots of physical abuse and putting her foot down his throat, eventually ending in her killing him by letting him bleed to death after the abuse. Sometimes he would want to die at the hands of the guy she was secretively fucking.

On a similar note, I had one guy tell me his wife was sleeping with another man and he had heard her say he wanted to kill her husband (the caller). His fantasy would be that he wanted me to play his wife and torture and kill him. The entire time I was torturing him, I would tell him how worthless he was and how I would rather fuck my boyfriend then him and that I was going to make it look like a suicide so that I would get all the life insurance. The sad part is, he'd cum just as you'd say you were "squeezing the life out of him." Each time I talked to him, the way he wanted to die would be different.

Another caller would also climax as I was talking about squeezing the life out of him, or some such words. He wanted me to hang a noose in the bedroom, put him on it, but slowly pull him up, letting it get tighter and tighter. All the while, he would be getting fucked by big black men. He wanted me to explain how I would pull hard, "snuffing" the life out of him, and then release him, letting him breath again, only to be impaled on the big black dick once more.

And of course, I was to be calling him names and humiliating him. He was only allowed to cum at the very second I killed him.

Miscellaneous

I talked to one guy who was gay and had HIV and told me that he would go out and have unprotected sex with his partners on purpose. At least he was telling them he had HIV beforehand so they knew they were putting themselves at risk when they had sex with him, but still! I thought that was horrible and really gave gay men a bad name. Although, most of the guys I talk to give straight men a bad name too!

One guy had a very specific fantasy every time, it was, verbatim, to "rape his big breasted mother while his daughter watches, then vice versa." It was the same every time, starting out by talking about fucking one while the other watched, then switching half way through.

Gary was a great money maker, because he would talk for hours on end, however he was a bit of a pain in the butt because he would whisper. Why would he whisper you ask? Because his family was in the next room! Every once in awhile, a family member would walk in and interrupt him, sadly, usually his kids. He would say "I'm on the phone with your uncle, I'll be done in a minute." Five hours later, and being interrupted three more times, he might be done, or he'd move onto another girl for five more hours.

His fantasy was somewhat simple: he wanted to snort cocaine and talk about fucking every member of my family. We would snort cocaine off of everyone. I was obviously not snorting cocaine and I doubt he was either, because if we honestly sniffed as much cocaine as he said we did during each call, we'd be dead in the first ten minutes!

So one night we are talking and Gary says he's in his car outside, because it's really early in the morning and he didn't want to wake anyone by doing the call inside. So he parked his car two houses down to be less suspicious if his wife came out. How is that less suspicious? Anyway, so he's sitting in his car for about four hours when I hear a knock on his window. He asks me to hold on and he puts the phone down, and I could hear everything that was going on. Needless to say, a policeman knocked on his window, because his neighbors called them about a suspicious car parked in front of their house for hours, with a man inside.

Now, at this point, my mouth drops, then when he answers the policeman about why he's there he says "I couldn't sleep and was just sitting in my car listening to music." Of course the cop asks, "Why can't you do that in your driveway?" And he said he didn't want to wake his wife. Now I have muted my phone so I can crack up laughing! Why didn't he just tell the officer that he was jerking off and didn't want to get caught?! I think the cop would have been fine with that, but instead, he came up with this stupid story which made the cop even more suspicious. The funniest thing is that he left me on hold the whole ten minutes while the cop was questioning him! It wouldn't have surprised me if Gary continued to talk to me after that, unfortunately he did not.

Along similar lines of being interrupted, this one call with Colin had me laughing hysterically! We would talk every few days for only about ten minutes at a time, and he would whisper too because someone was in the house. So one time, I'm on the phone with him and this woman interrupts after a few minutes with: "Colin, you little bitch! What are you doing?" and she says it with a very, umm, well, animated attitude if you catch my drift. I was completely silent, and so was he. We were both caught off guard and when he finally spoke, he said he wasn't doing anything. Hello!? Like she's going to believe that one! Obviously, she heard us talking and knew what was going on. I love people who are caught in the act, know they are caught, and STILL lie! I honestly didn't expect to hear back from him again, but he did call me back about a month later. I of course asked if he was still with his girl, and he said yes, she got over it.

There was this one guy who was just completely off the wall and from left field. This is one of those guys that you really are wondering: "Where did this fantasy come from!?" It started out as a straight sex call talking about how we were just going to fuck, then when he was somewhat close to cumming, he asked me to say: "I want to eat your liquid babies for Satan and not for Jesus." And he made me say it over and over again, nothing else, for the last two minutes of the call, until he came. Now explain that one to me!

CHAPTER SIX:
Why They Are The Way They Are

One of the first things someone asks me when I tell them about a really off the wall fantasy is: "Where does that come from? Why are they into that?" That question is so hard to answer unless a caller comes straight out and tells me. However, I have come out and asked some clients why they like what they like, and I feel they have given me a straight answer, and therefore, sometimes I am able to answer that question. To be honest, there are a lot of clients who actually enjoy telling me where their specific fantasy came from and how it developed. I think it's another way to relive the fantasy in a different way.

Sometimes I wish I was a psychologist and could really analyze them, however, I have been told by my clients that I do a great job playing psychologist for them when they want it. I've even had clients ask me where I think their fantasy comes from, because even *they* have no idea. And I'll ask them questions, and they are amazed at how I'm able to bring things out of them, and ask questions they've never been asked before.

I am not necessarily someone who is qualified to analyze the inner workings of the psyche. I am not a psychologist, someone educated in psychology or even a criminologist. However, how do people become an expert in their fields? Some through education and others through experience, I believe I fall into the latter category. While my experience spans only seven years (at the writing of this book), I have extensive knowledge of virtually all fetishes and have talked to many phone sex callers about where their fantasies come from. Now I understand that each person is different, but below you'll find some of the explanations that my callers have given to me.

In previous chapters, I discussed some callers who were pretty interesting, and below I'm going to revisit some of those callers and talk about what they've told me and my analysis of them based on their fantasies.

Pantyhose girl's story is interesting as to where it comes from. To remind you about "her", he's the one who likes to wear his pantyhose on the top and bottom half of his body.

He said he grew up in a religious family and they would go to church and all the women in his family always wore pantyhose. He told me that being young, before he can walk, because he was at that height, he could remember staring at their legs in pantyhose. His mother even told him that when he was a kid he would touch her pantyhose covered legs all the time. She even told him he could touch her legs when she wore pantyhose any time he wanted. So in some aspects, she fed into his fantasy, even though she had no idea what it would do to him later.

When he got older, he would steal his mother's pantyhose and wear them. He wouldn't just wear them, he would sit in his pantyhose and think about all the girls and women he knew who wore pantyhose and wondered why they chose the color, style, or brand that they did. These thoughts started his obsession of finding the perfect pair of pantyhose. And that's exactly what he did. He has had one of every different type and style of pantyhose and now has a specific type that really turns him on.

He told me that once the internet came along, his fetish grew exponentially because he had access to pantyhose fetish sites and was able to learn more about all different types of pantyhose as well as explore his fantasy even more. These websites also made him feel more comfortable with his fetish. There were more people out there besides him who had his same or similar obsession.

I think that although Pantyhose Girl likes to be called a faggot and teased and made fun of for his love of pantyhose, and while he does use a dildo in his ass, I don't think he's gay or bi. He has no urge to be with a man at all. My thought is that his fetish started with the pure sensation of the smooth and silky touch of pantyhose. We all have something that feels good when we touch it; he just took his to another level.

It could be that because he loved the feel of pantyhose so much that he tried them on, and because he wore them, thought that he wanted to be a girl and maybe for a time questioned his sexuality, I do not know. However, I know from talking to him that his main focus of what gets him going is talking about the feel of pantyhose, on himself and on me. He asks me to tell him over and over again how it's okay that he can touch my pantyhose whenever he wants. I think the other things, like the dildos and being teased is just a side note to the fantasy.

Now while I hate to think about Larry any more, the guy who made me rethink becoming a phone sex operator, his fantasy makes you wonder where such a sick fantasy comes from. The only insight I have with him is some other stories he told me while we talked.

He once said that he would hire prostitutes to come to his hotel room and when they agreed to do whatever he wanted, he'd tie them up and torture them so badly that they'd cry. He told me that he even made one girl quit. This just shows how his fantasy has escalated over time. He said he was doing phone sex, but that it wasn't enough and he started to do some of it to the prostitutes. While I do not know where his fantasies originated, it's interesting to delve into these other details more. It also makes you wonder if he'd take it even further than he already had.

He obviously has some hatred to women to want to torture them so badly. In fact, now that I think about it, I do not remember him ever saying why he wanted to torture me. It just seemed to be because he could, because I had nowhere else to go and therefore had to take it. Sounds like a classic abuser, using his power to dominate, manipulate, and control the women in his life.

Along with the above, I also believe that with the amount of graphic details in his story, that he really did have some animosity toward the man with whom he wanted me kill at the end of his fantasy. It worried me that he might actually go through with hurting him and I would never know. Which is always a hazard when dealing with guys with this type of fantasy?

Another client of mine who has been a client since I started phone sex, has a very interesting story. Carl L, the one who wanted to be beaten up, called me one day and told me how he walked into his neighbor's house to steal her panties and she walked in on him. The door was unlocked, but no car in the driveway, so he thought she wasn't home. So when she suddenly appeared in the hallway, he froze and then made up some lame excuse as to why he had to come into her home unannounced.

He had talked before about how he loved his neighbor's panties that she hung on her clothing line outside. And it shocked me that he took the next step from admiring the panties to panty raiding. I would joke to him all the time that he should go and steal some off the line if she ever kept them over night, but he said she didn't. Let me also clarify something, I'm sure some people are thinking: "Who hangs their panties on a cloths line?" she was in her 70's, so that may help explain things a little.

From what I knew about his personal history, he is currently in his early fifties and his father had passed away 10 years prior. He was then forced to live at home and take care of his mother until she passed away a few years later. He was never married and never had a serious girlfriend and worked a menial job. He drank heavily and was buried in debt. Although it didn't surprise me that he wanted to steal her panties, it did surprise me that he actually went through with it.

After he told me what he had done, I asked him a few questions. First was: "Have you ever thought about hurting a woman?" His answer was an emphatic "No". My second question was: "Was your mother overbearing and did she not like the idea of you being with women?" His answer was an definite "Yes", and my last question was: "Do you ever fantasizing about hurting your mother?" His answer to this question was "No, I loved my mother, but I do have a lot of animosity towards her." I had a feeling he'd say no to my first question, but definitely wasn't surprised by his other answers. Just based on what I've read from my criminal justice books, it doesn't surprise me that his mother was overbearing and didn't want him to be with woman, and that's why he was living in the same house he grew up in and had never really dated. In fact, it wouldn't surprise me if his mother's room was left exactly the same as it did when she died.

To be completely honest, I am waiting for him to show up on the news as a serial killer. While I am no criminal profiler, I bet if I delved deeper, I'd find out that he was a late bedwetter and a pyromaniac when he was a child. Of course I don't think he has ever tortured animals, because he talks so lovingly about his cat. The reason I mention these is because these three things make up the Homicidal Triad, which most serial killer have. He happens to be a really sweet guy, but isn't that what all the neighbors of serial killer say?

Regarding other less severe fantasies, I have talked to two different adult babies who have said they didn't start their fantasy till way later in life. They explained that their girlfriends put them in diapers as a roleplay during sex and after they broke up, they just kept wearing them. They had for so long equating being in diapers to being turned on that it just stuck with them.

But then I talked to another adult baby who said he wet his bed until he was 13 years old and therefore, had to sleep in diapers growing up. He said that he didn't have any sexual fantasies at the time, and in fact, those fantasies didn't develop till he was 21 years old. He just liked to be put in a diaper and teased. He said that it probably developed from his sister, who would sometimes change him up until about age 10, but then would tease him about wetting his bed. It was this constant teasing that probably led to his sexual fantasies.

Another diaper boy actually went as far as buying hypnotic tapes designed specifically for Adult Baby/Diaper Lovers (ABDL). (Who knew they made such a thing!?). He listened to them every night before bed and while sleeping. These tapes would give him the need and encouragement to wet the bed. They were designed so that when you stopped using the tapes, you would wet the bed naturally and subconsciously, and therefore, be forced to wear diapers to bed. He told me after he finished those tapes; he would soon listen to the ones that would force you to pee subconsciously while you were awake too.

———————

Queer boy says that him wanting to be verbally abused and blackmailed comes from the fact that he was a very skinny late bloomer with a tiny dick. Because of the skinny late bloomer, he was constantly teased by girls all throughout school. It doesn't help now that the medication he's on forces him to not be able to get an erection. Interestingly enough, he says he even fantasized as early as elementary school about girls tying him up naked and making fun of him.

His home life isn't that great either. While he does have a family, he sleeps in a separate room from his wife. They get along, but not physically or sexually. With me, the constant berating, threatening to out him, and forcing him to become a faggot is what turns him on and gets him off. While he is on this medication, he doesn't get an erection, but he's still able to ejaculate. Of course this fact gives even more fuel to the fire for me.

———————

One of my cross dressing clients said his desire to cross dress started because his older sister would force him into her clothing and make him play dress up with her since he was five years old. The constant being in women's clothing evolved into him wanting to wear it all the time. While most people don't realize that some children are really always developing sexually in their bodies. The children themselves may not be aware that their minds are processing these actions in a different way then their bodies. On the outside, wearing the woman's clothing was embarrassing and humiliating to him, but in his brain, it was being stored as a sexual exercise for later. In fact, he even said it wasn't until he was 14 years old that he tried on woman's clothing again, which brought him back to feeling humiliated and which turned him on.

———————

Jeff T. likes to wear nylon pantyhose and be bent over the knee or a bed by a woman wearing nylon pantyhose, and spanked with a hand or leather strap. I asked him where this all came from and his answer was that while he was in his sexual development, around age seven, his mother would bend him over her knee in her chair when he would do something wrong, always wearing her nylon pantyhose, and paddle his butt with a leather strap. His fantasy does not involve his mother or a mother-like figure, and he's adamant about telling me it has nothing to do with her specifically. It's just that while he was rubbing against her legs and getting spanked, he would get turned on. It just happened to be at a time when his sexual development was in full swing. Needless to say, the only way for him to have the best orgasms, is for him to replay this scenario. His one interesting thing is that he only likes to be punished when he's actually done something wrong, and have the woman roleplay that they are going to punish him for that one thing.

It really is interesting how a little moment in a person's life can affect him years later. And more interesting is how it affects some people and not others. How is it that two people can be forced to play dress up with their sisters and only one come out wanting to cross dress?

This answer, I hope, will become another book, where we can really delve deeper into their psyche and talk to psychologists and criminologists who might be able to explain these weird fetishes.

CHAPTER SEVEN:
Shedding the Light

Do you get turned on?

This is probably the first question guys used to ask me when I told them what I do for a living. The answer is a flat out NO. The honest answer is that the calls I take are so messed up and perverted that I'm glad it doesn't turn me on. Not that it's necessarily "wrong" to have the fantasies some callers have, but it's just that they are a little more kinky than what I am into. Now, to be honest, I do get some guys who are attractive, jerking their dick in front of me on cam, and are just talking about how they love to have me watch them jack off and talk about how I'd make them cum. But I am still not turned on by them. I guess in some respects, I'm numb to all of that at this point, and I find it hard to get turned on to any of the callers, nor do I want to, for me, it's just a job. And again, it's not "wrong" for them to be calling a phone sex line. It's just not something that turns me on as an individual.

At one point in my life I had considered becoming a BDSM Mistress/Dominatrix. A lot of the guys who call me for feminization ask me if I would do it in person. I don't, but the fantasies are straight forward and seem easy. The guys don't want to have sex with you; they want to worship you. And sometimes, it goes one better: As an example, they want to be your sissy maid and feel pathetic being dressed in a maid's outfit and forced to clean your house while you watch. At the time, I figured, I can do that easy! So I talked to a few real-time Mistresses that I knew, and they said that unless you get aroused by them licking your boots, or dressing them up, or even fucking them with strap-ons, then you shouldn't do it real-time. Well, that wasn't going to happen, so that idea flew out the window.

However, I do not feel that phone sex and being a dominatrix are the same. I do not get turned on by my calls, but I am ranked up in the community as one of the best. None of my friends who are phone sex operators get turned on by it either. So, the long answer is no, you don't have to get turned on by phone sex to actually do it. You just need to be creative, open minded, and willing to please.

Have you ever thought about escorting?

Sometimes I'll get a caller asking to meet me. What I tell him depends on him, the caller. If I do say yes, it's in an attempt to get him to call back again, knowing that if I say no, he won't call back. Knowing full well that me meeting them will never happen, I just string them along.

Then I have clients who ask to meet under the argument that phone sex is the same as escorting, so why won't I do it? I get pissed off when I hear that one. Phone sex does not equate to escorting. While I am helping someone get off, I am in no way meeting them or coming in contact with them physically. However, I don't look down upon people who escort—I say more power to you! But it is definitely not for me. I have no urge to have physical contact with any of my clients, or get paid to have sex with them. It ties into the question of being turned on, and as the answer is no, I doubt getting paid for sex would either.

Would you be upset if your husband called phone sex?

While it may seem like a "Catch 22", yes, I would be upset if my husband called for phone sex, for two reasons. One, if he's doing it without telling me and therefore hiding something from me, and two, because it would indicate I've done something wrong or am lacking something sexually for him. The guys who call me to jack off do so because their significant other isn't into their fantasy and won't do it, they just haven't told them about their fantasy, or they aren't having sex with them at all—all factors of miscommunication. I feel that my husband and I have a very open relationship in regards to our feelings—we tell each other everything. Therefore, if my husband was calling for phone sex, it means he isn't being honest with me. I ask him about his fantasies—I tell him he can tell me anything and I won't react negatively. Again, if he's calling phone sex lines to masturbate, then I'm not doing something right or giving him all the sex he needs—essentially, we're not communicating correctly. And I pride myself on being open to trying new things. If I'm not interested, it's not because I'm judging, it's because it just doesn't turn me on. So he has no reason not to tell me he's interested in trying something out. He should never feel he has to call someone else to tell a fantasy to.

Do they feel it's cheating to call you?

Considering the answer to the above question, I do feel that it is cheating to some extent when you call a phone sex operator without your significant other being aware of it. However, I tell my clients that it's not. Again, it's simply a matter of economics in that respect: I get their cash if I relieve them of their guilt. But I do believe to a certain extent that they should feel okay with telling me their fantasies—these fantasies they can't share with someone else for whatever reason. It is a bit of a dichotomy and a double standard on my end. I tell them they shouldn't feel guilty for playing with themselves and cumming while talking to me. Sometimes I tell them it's better than actually having sex with someone else and cheating that way. But mostly what I focus on is that there's no physical penetration or contact with a phone sex operator, nor are there any feelings (on average). Thus, it's not cheating for them.

How does it affect your sex life?

At first, I felt really guilty if my boyfriends were over, and we were planning on having sex and a call came in. Not only did it interrupt our time together, but sometimes it would throw off my boyfriend, especially if he heard me responding to someone wanting to, say, fuck my ass. Usually, though, my guilt came from having sex after the call. I didn't want my boyfriend to think that it was the call that had turned me on and not him. I tried to not let it affect my sex life and would ignore those feelings of guilt. On the flip side, I had a few boyfriends who didn't even want to be around when I was taking calls, so it didn't affect our sex lives at all. It really wasn't until I started doing phone sex full time after I was married that I sat down with my husband to discuss how my phone sex life would affect our life together.

At first, he was turned off by my callers and really didn't want to have sex if I had just taken a call. Once we sat down and discussed that, no matter what, it wasn't the calls that got us turned on—that it was each other—we were able to get past all of that. Say we were planning on having sex, were fooling around in bed, and I hadn't signed off of work to stop getting calls, and the phone rang; needless to say, I'm already wet, and I do a call about a guy who wants to see me fuck a dog. But when I hang up, my husband and I are still going to have sex, because the two of us just let it go in one ear and out the other. It just doesn't affect us anymore, and we have a very healthy sex life.

What kind of legally questionable situations have you encountered?

I've been asked a ton of times if I've ever called the police after a guy has talked about a certain fantasy. To be honest, yes, twice. The first time I called the police was after a call I had taken in my first year. While I normally didn't know the guy's information, the company I worked for would give its PSOs the guy's last name so that we could keep track of our callers. During the call, he told me what town he lived in. He had a fantasy about a VERY young girl and said that he actually did it, that it wasn't a fantasy. Needless to say, I hung up before the call was technically over. I signed off work and paced back and forth in my bedroom, debating what I should do.

Eventually, I went online and looked up the police department for that city, and I called the non-emergency line and talked to an officer. His reaction was more along the lines of, "You do what?" He definitely didn't take me seriously. Not that the officer laughed per se, but it was obvious he could care less. He told me there was nothing they could do because there was no way to prove the caller actually did anything wrong. First, it was only hearsay—they would have to investigate based on what a phone sex operator said. Second, because he didn't admit it in a recording, or in person, and he didn't give a name of the girl he molested, they had nothing to work on. Case closed.

I hung up the phone, very disappointed and feeling horrible that there was nothing I could do. I really had to sit down and think about how I would deal with another call like that—I didn't have any illusions that it wouldn't happen again. After awhile, I realized that, most likely, the guy was lying about what he had done, and that it was all probably part of his fantasy. From that day forward, for any call I had, I had to take whatever the caller said as fantasy and couldn't let it bother me—very similar to the hard lesson I learned with Larry.

I never called the police again until a few years later. A guy called me, and while we were on the call, which was very vanilla, I could hear in the background, "Daddy, let me out" and banging on a door. I stopped talking for a moment to make sure I wasn't imagining it. And then I heard it again: the banging and, "Daddy, let me out." The guy said nothing, just dear air punctuated by banging and pleading, so I asked, "What was that?" while trying to keep my voice steady, calm. He paused a moment and then said, "Nobody, just my dog." I slammed down the receiver and called the police. Luckily, I had his address, phone number, and last name because he'd called my own company. I called the non-emergency line once again, but it went to a policeman's voicemail. I told him that I was a phone sex operator and gave a description of what I'd heard. I gave all the caller's information and asked if the police would call me back if they investigated. Needless to say, I never received a call back.

That is the only other situation I've come across in which I've felt the need to call the police. I think the only other situation would be if someone said they had killed someone and said exactly where the body was buried or named who they killed. Or well, if they said the name of the child they molested or the person they had raped. And of course, if I had all their information to inform police with.

While I've had calls that have certainly made me question humanity and that person's morality, and well, sometimes my own, I always just let it roll off my back.

I recently had a problem with a client who went one step too far with his obsessive fantasy, which caused me to take action. Steve M. has been a client of mine for the last six or so years. He didn't call as much, but emailed and I charged him per email. He had been obsessed with this woman he had met through the company he works for. He met her for only one day, fifteen years ago. Since that day, he has been completely obsessed with her. The reason he only met her for one day was because they were on a company outing and he arrived a day before her group was leaving. They both work for a large corporation that has regional offices throughout the United States. He talked to her on a somewhat regular basis for the first year, then I'm sure she thought he was creepy and rarely kept in touch.

From the day they met, to fifteen years later, he had been calling various phone sex agencies, asking for psychics to talk to about her. Come on, who calls a phone sex agency for a psychic? His emails and phone conversations were the same, all the time, and I'm talking about two emails a day asking the same questions in different ways. Each time he would find out new information about her, he would tell the psychic to comment on it. From marriage to pregnancy, he was obsessed with her tits and pussy being used over and over again. How stretched out and saggy she was.

That was all fine and dandy, however boring it was, I could deal with it. He lived in another state that her, and always had, so I wasn't too worried. I feared for the day that he moved to the same state, because then, I knew he would stalk her. I hoped it would never come to the point where I'd have to call her, but had a feeling it probably would. I was smart that over the years he had given out various clues about her, so that when I went on his MySpace page, years ago, it wasn't hard to find her. Needless to say, it was really easy to "predict" things about her, having access to her social networking page. Then, recently, he emailed me about how he had just gotten access to the company's personnel files and some other things, and looked up all sorts of medical and personal information about her. That pushed it over the edge.

Now he was looking at confidential records, which is illegal. Needless to say, when I got that email, I knew I had to call her, so I did.

My mind was racing as to how to just introduce myself and get her to talk to me. Well I had to go through a few people, but when I mentioned his name, they immediately gave me her phone number. It seems she had been having problems with this guy constantly contacting her anyway. I called her and told her who I was and how he had been obsessed since that one day and told her some vague details about what we talked about, telling her that I preferred not having to go into detail. I stumbled through the first half of the call (the whole call only lasting about ten minutes). She was surprisingly calm, but obviously frustrated and annoyed, thankfully not at me. I told her I wanted my name left out of it, but that she could call me if she needed more information. Thankfully, the company keeps strict record of who does what with their log ins, so they should have a record that shows what he actually looked up, so I hope they won't need to contact me. But let me tell you, I wish I had never had to do any of this, and that it just stayed to good old fashioned fantasy! I guess after 15 years, he had to bring it to new heights. I haven't heard anything back from her, and it's been at least a month since I contacted her.

How does your significant other react to it?

When I was single, and I met a guy and I told them what I did for a living, that I was a phone sex operator, they would say "that's so cool! Can I listen?" And I'd say "sure, but it's not like what you think." I think they thought they would be watching me masturbate while I was talking about fucking someone else. Or that I would fuck them while I talked to a guy. To be honest, I am not even remotely turned on by my callers, and don't like to associate my sex life with my career. Not saying that it's wrong if some PSO's do, I just don't.

So then I'd tell them the type of calls I did. They changed their mind real quickly about listening! In fact, every guy I dated never wanted to be around me when I did a call, unless it was a "normal" one. Well, you never know what type of call you're going to get, so that meant I only worked when I wasn't around them.

I've probably mentioned this in another question, but my husband, since the beginning hasn't been bothered by the calls. He knows they are all fantasy, he knows I do not get off to them, and therefore, he just ignores them. In fact, he's one of those people who can tune everything out around him if he needs to. If he doesn't like the fantasy, he'll either do that or go into another room. If I am doing a fantasy that I feel might make him uncomfortable, I will go into the other room to do the call. For example, I do not like doing rape calls in front of him, actually makes me feel bad for some reason. He doesn't care one way or another, like I said, he tunes it all out.

He is like me, after the call, he doesn't remember what happened because he just lets it go in one ear out the other. If we dwelled on it for longer than that, we'd go crazy!

How did your parents react?

The whole situation of my parents finding out was really quite interesting. It started out with my father coming out to Las Vegas, where I was living at the time. I was somewhat struggling and he told me I had to get a second job. I told him I had one already and for him to not worry. He kept pushing, but I wouldn't tell him what it was, and of course he thought I was a prostitute, so I had to tell him I did phone sex. His first comment was, "oh . . . don't' tell your mother."

My mother knew I worked as a dispatcher for a phone sex company and when she found out how much money the operators were making she went to my dad and said, "What would you say if our daughter did phone sex." Obviously, she wasn't upset! Needless to say, years later, my mom would mail me panties she found really cheap, knowing I could sell them. Her letter to me would say, "Found these panties. Thought someone would buy them." Tell me that isn't great!

Do you often tell people what you do for a living?

When I first started doing phone sex, I didn't tell anyone. I was a little embarrassed, more so at what they might think of it. Then, after I started doing it full time, I told anyone who asked me. Honestly, it's a totally legal and legit profession, why should I be ashamed of what I do? I mean, I really love what I do, I get to work from home and work whatever hours I want. It's perfect! And now that I own my own company, I'm really proud of what I do. And look, now even a book!

However, I have come across some situations where I will lie about it. For example, if my husband doesn't feel that someone he works for will appreciate having someone working for them with a wife who does phone sex, I tell him to just lie and say I'm in customer service. For the most part, the people he works for love the fact that I do it and find it really interesting. Also, I have volunteered at some places where I have been hesitant to say what I do, in fear that they will look at me differently, or that they'll feel that me working for them will put a negative light on their organization. Every person is different, and I have to judge them each differently.

When I my husband and I first got together, we didn't tell his parents for fear of their reaction. Now they are fine with it.

How much do you make, bottom line?

Bottom line? Now that's a tough one. I make about $50,000 a year. I do phone sex calls and run my own business, however, at this present moment, I do not take money out of the business, but instead, put it back into it for advertising and expansion. I only pay myself for what I work. I get paid about $.55/minute to earn the $50,000 a year. Some years it's less, some more.

Does it make you question humanity?

Honestly, no, it doesn't make me question humanity per say. I get asked all the time if when I walk around and look at each person and think, "Wow, I wonder if they are into some of the messed up shit I hear." I don't really. If I did, I think I would go crazy and never trust anyone. Sometimes however, I will joke to someone and say, "Oh, I bet he likes to be peed on," as we walk by a guy. Now, while I'm someone who doesn't want children to begin with, my doing phone sex makes me not want them more. I talk to a lot of guys who could be would-be pedophiles if they stopped taking their sexual frustration out on me. To be a mother would make me fear letting my child out by themselves, or definitely never let them have a babysitter.

Do you talk to women?

This is a real easy question to answer. I have been doing phone sex for about 7 years, and in that time, I have only talked to 3 women by themselves and another 2 with another guy on the line.

The reason that I think women don't call phone sex is because women are more visual then auditory. And, we also don't, on average, have as high a sex drive as men. I'm sure men get bored jacking off all the time to the same thing, so they need change.

And to be blatantly honest, I think women are smart enough to know that the person on the other end doesn't look like the model picture they have in their ad, and that they aren't masturbating

How many people a day do you talk to?

I talk to about 10-20 people a day and average $100-150 per day in income. Now, some months can be much worse than others. But I work all the time, literally 24/7, unless my husband has a day off and then I actually take some time for us. But I work in the middle of the night. I'm a light sleeper, and if a phone call comes in at 4am, I'm there to take it.

It sounds horrible and hectic, but as I've said before, I'm money driven. Since, at the writing of this book, my company is still only finishing it's second year—but doing really well thankfully—I am doing most of the dispatching as well. I hope in the next year, that I will be able to do one of two things; either stop doing phone sex—unless absolutely needed, and for my regulars—and just dispatch, or only do phone sex and hire someone to dispatch for me.

How can you do something so personal via such an impersonal mode of communication?—OR—How can you do these things with people you don't even know?

To be honest, this is an easier question to answer then one might think. I'm sure most people reading this book have had phone sex with a significant other, and you're thinking, "But that's different, I know this person, I've seen them or I've been with them before." And while that is true, I can do the same thing with another guy by letting him believe it's like we are together. I make the guy feel comfortable, I ask him what he looks like, so I can picture it in my head, I ask him to tell me what he's doing so I can imagine him doing it and therefore respond accordingly. I need to be able to see every aspect of what he's doing and to really get into his head in order to make him do exactly what he needs to feel the best.

When I first started phone sex, I would just imagine what I've done to past boyfriends. Now, because it just comes so naturally, I don't even think about what I am doing with these guys. It's almost as if the words just come out of my mouth and I am not in control of it.

Also, I don't find this personal on my end. While I know it's very personal on the guys end, because they are touching their body and making themselves orgasm, it isn't personal. But as I stated, to make it personal, I make them feel like I'm there with them. In fact, one of my lines is: "Close your eyes and imagine I'm there with you, that it's my hand . . ." That really helps, putting yourself in front of them in their mind. And while watching someone on cam do something is a lot more personal, the guys who are calling phone sex are more audibly aroused. Meaning that they are more turned on by the way a girl's voice sounds, more so than what they look like. I am sure most guys know that the pictures on most girls websites are not them, but they can block that all out by listening to their voices.

How many other women, that you know of, have met their clients?

I actually only know of one other girl, besides myself, who have met their clients. One was actually one of my girls (the operators who work for me) and she was lucky things ended like they did. I of course was forced to fire her, because she, Chloe, signed a contract with me that strictly prohibits contact with clients. If there is, it will result in being let go. While I decided to meet a client that had a normal fantasy, which I don't condone, she decided to meet a client of hers that had some of the sickest fantasies I've heard.

The only reason I knew she met him was because her client called another one of my girls and told her. I then listened in on the call the next time he called for Chloe. I got to hear bits and pieces of what had happened. Thankfully, he wanted only sex and not to act out one of his perverted fantasies. He called my company to meet up with him again, because she wasn't answering her cell phone. Thankfully, she had realized the error in her ways and decided to not meet with him again (or so she said on the phone). I have no idea what happened when they met up and am very thankful she decided to not do it again.

CHAPTER EIGHT:
"Taboo" Sex Definitions

You know how you can type into an internet search engine: "weird laws" and get some crazy laws all over the country that are still on the books, laws you never knew existed? Well it's the same way with sex. There are so many different types of things that people masturbate to, some you will stop and have to do a double take. Here are some I thought might interest you.

*Definitions from www.Bondage.com and
www.TheFetishList.com*

Abrasion—Having your partner scratch, scrape or bruise your skin.

Acrophilia—Being aroused by sexual activities at unusual heights. Most common is having sex on a balcony, while sitting on the railing with your legs wrapped around your partner

Agalmatophilia—Being aroused by statues. This fetish may or may not involve actual sexual acts with statues.

Analingus—Licking your partner's asshole for pleasure, also known as "rim jobs" or "tossing the salad."

Asphyxiation—Temporarily preventing the flow of oxygen to the lungs. Usually done via choking with hands.

Autocunnilingus—The act of a woman giving herself oral sex.

Autofellatio—The act of sucking one's own penis.

Autopederasty—The act of sticking one's own erect penis in one's own rectum. Amazingly enough, there is a small percentage of people who can do it.

Barosmia—Being aroused from smells.

Bestiality—Wanting to have sex with an animal.

Boot Worship—Worshiping via licking, sucking, and cleaning with the mouth, your dominant partner's boots. This is also similar to Heel or Shoe Worship. Many people want the boots to be dirty first.

Boxing/Closeting—The act of being put in a box or closet. A form of deprivation.

Caning—Being hit with a cane—a long, thin, and flexible implement. Besides pain, it can cause intense arousal and can be used for punishment.

Catheterization—Using a Catheter (used by hospitals inside your urethra/peehole for you to pee out of when you can't pee by yourself). Catheters are usually used to dilate your urethra for stimulation.

CBT: Cock and Ball Torture—Torturing the cock and ball using various objects. Usually does not including permanent damage. May include, but not limited to crushing balls, smacking balls or cock, using clothes pins, nipple clamps, paddles, and insertion of objects into the urethra.

Chastity Belts—Using a devise on the genitals to prevent sexual intercourse and arousal (for men). Not necessarily having a belt attached. They are fully functioning to go about your day to day activities and are quite easily hidden.

Collars and Leashes—Made for the submissive partner to wear and be walked around like a puppy dog. Collars can also signify ownership.

Corophilia—Receiving sexual pleasure by using feces.

Crucifixion—Affixing someone to a cross, or cross-like object

Dendrophilia—Being aroused by trees.

Emetophilia—Becoming aroused and orgasms while throwing up or while watching someone throw up.

Enemas—Giving your partner an "Enema"—an apparatus used for injecting liquid into the intestine by way of the anus, often for the purposes of cleansing.

Fluffies—Dressing up like a giant stuffed animal or mascot

Forniphilia—Fetish involving strapping someone into the shape of furniture.

Gun Play—Using guns as props in your sexual play.

Infantilism—Becoming aroused by dressing up or being dressed up like a baby. Sometimes being treated like one, coddled, including breast feeding and diaper changing.

Klismaphilia—Getting aroused from getting an enema. An Enema is when water is inserted into your rectum, usually to clean you out inside.

Knife Play—Lightly running a knife along your partner's body without necessarily cutting them.

Lactophilia—Being aroused to breast milk

Macrophilia—Attraction to giants, being men or women.

Mumification—Wrapping your partner in cloth to make them completely immobile and look like a mummy.

Nyotaimori—Eating sushi off a naked person's body.

Plastic Wrap—Wrapping your partner or being wrapped in plastic wrap. Used as a form of bondage.

Pony Play—Pretending to be a pony and having someone ride you, including saddle, reins, crop, etc.

Pseudonecrophilia—This is where your partner pretends to be dead while you are having sex with them. Unlike Necrophilia, this is actually legal.

Puppy Play—Having a sub behave and appear like a puppy, and treating them as such.

PVC—Enjoying the smell, feel, and look of PVC on your own person. "PVC" refers to Polyvinylchloride, a thermoplastic polymer.

Roman Shower—Becoming aroused to someone throwing up on you.

Sensory Deprivation—Blocking or limiting the sensory input your partner receives. Using blindfolds, earplugs, hoods, etc.

Sounds—Sounds are devices that go inside to "explore" a part of your body. Urethra sounds are long skinny, usually metal objects that go inside the urethra of the penis (the pee hole).

Speculums—A medical device used to spread and dilate the vagina while at a gynecologist. Used for both anal and vaginal entry during sexual acts.

Swinging—Swapping partners with another couple.

Teledildonics—Also known as Dildonics, is the computer software or hardware used to aid remote sex between two or more people.

Teratophilia—Being aroused by people who are deformed. There are different types of Teratophilia, one being acrotomophilia, which is being aroused by amputees

Toucherism—Needing to touch your penis or vagina against another person.